The Great American Baseball Card Flipping, Trading and Bubble Gum Book

LUKE EASTER

BASEBALL THRILLS

MAYS' CATCH MAKES SERIES HISTORY

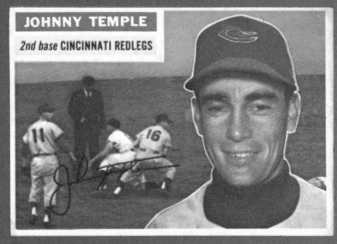

JOHNNY TEMPLE

2nd base CINCINNATI REDLEGS

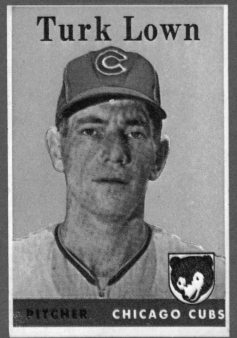

Turk Lown

PITCHER   CHICAGO CUBS

565 FEET

MANTLE BLASTS
565 FT. HOME RUN

The Great American Baseball Card Flipping, Trading and Bubble Gum Book

Brendan C. Boyd
and Fred C. Harris

A Sports Illustrated Book

Little, Brown and Company — Boston - Toronto

this book is for
Joan and Gail

First Edition

T 09/73

The authors are grateful to Topps Baseball Cards for permission to reprint the pictures in this book. Copyright Topps Chewing Gum, Incorporated, Brooklyn, N. Y.

*Sports Illustrated Books
are published by
Little, Brown and Company
in association with
Sports Illustrated Magazine*

Library of Congress Cataloging in Publication Data

Boyd, Brendan C
   The great American baseball card flipping, trading,
and bubble gum book.

   "A Sports illustrated book."
   1. Baseball cards. I. Harris, Fred C., 1943-
joint author. II. Title.
GV875.2.B69   769'.4'2   73-12826
ISBN 0-316-10429-9

Published simultaneously in Canada by Little, Brown & Company (Canada) Limited

Printed in the United States of America

Acknowledgments

I don't know how you happen to feel about this, but I like to read a book through entirely. Stem to stern. Cover to cover. From the first faint digits of the copyright to the final florid lines of the jacket copy. Slowly. Carefully. Lovingly. Forewords and Acknowledgments. Footnotes and Indexes. None of this reading dynamics business for me. Am I now alone in this curious custom?

I mean, are there still any of those patient souls left out there in the wilderness who delight in reading of the author's undying devotion to his dear old mum, his deep gratitude to the caretakers at the Ashmoleum Museum, his cloying hosannas to the keepers of the Guggenheim flame? To say nothing of those cryptically Byzantine dedications to cryptically Byzantine pals — "To Lollie and Sam, who danced with the Tiger without tripping on the stripes." "To Rocco and Nip, compulsive disentanglers of life's irrepressible embroglio." "To Moishe — who laughed." I mean who the hell reads this stuff anyway? Or understands it? Or even cares. Just me? (And you?)

Well, having said all this I must now proceed, alas, to my own list of thank-you notes, kudos, bouquets. Because I'm afraid it is only too true, after all is said and done, that no book, no matter how artless, could hope to exist without a whole passel of help from its friends; and that this book, unworthy as it is, would have been even more unworthy, might in fact not even have drawn first breath (which might not have been such a bad idea, come to think of it) had it not been for the kind and gracious help and encouragement of any number of kind and gracious persons.

Therefore:

Thank you Richard P. McDonough, boy manqué and editor extraordinaire, for ushering this troublesome child into the sunlight so tirelessly, so winningly, and so well. Thank you Sy Berger — Baseball King, Woody Gelman — Prime Minister of Nostalgia, Norman Liss — Press Agent to the World, for your time and your patience. Thank you Abner Doubleday for having invented baseball. Thank you Dwight Eisenhower for having invented the fifties. And thank you Richard Nixon for having brought it all back home. Thank you Joseph and Patricia Boyd for everything. And more. Thank you Thomas and Margaret Boyd for your critical assistance. Thank you Elizabeth Boyd and Frank Horrigan for anecdotes, wit, and wisdom. Thank you Elliott Caplin for professional and familial assistance. Thank you James Bishop, George and Rosalie Hickman, Tom Reed, Alan Pinkham, Glen Lewis, Gar Miller, John McLaughlin, and Donald George Caplin for your invaluable researches. Thank you Patti and Satchell Paige, a real fun couple if there ever was one, for being such great sports. Thank you Curt Gowdy and Chris Schenkel for giving us the inspiration to go on. Thank you professional baseball players everywhere—from Tommy Aaron to George Zuverink—for countless hours of enjoyment, relaxation, and even, occasionally, inspiration. And thank you Howard Cosell—just for being you.

And now for a few cautionary notes, or what Dr. Johnson might call an exhortatory aside.

Gentle Reader-

This book was conceived in love, nurtured in kindness, and brought forth into the world with a good healthy eye to the main chance. It was inspired by a plethora of motives and emotions too subtly cerebral and entangled to try and sort out here—not the least among them being vanity, ambition, and greed. But it was also written with a certain disrespectful reverence and a healthy longing for a more innocent and less troubled era. If you would enjoy it, as we hope you will, we urge on you the following prescription:

1) Do not, whatever else you might do, take any of it too seriously. It's only life after all. Although some people prefer to think of it as a game.

2) Please do not write us long, boring letters explaining that Herbie Plews batted .216 in 1954 and not .214 as we have stated, or that Don Ferrarese spells his name with 2 r's and 1 s. Frankly, we don't care.

3) Please do not write us equally long letters (especially threatening ones) complaining about how we have maligned your favorite ballplayer, belittled baseball, befouled the very air you breathe. We know only too well that we could not have played baseball half as well as even the most inept players mentioned herein. We know that much better than you, in fact. We tried.

4) Please wear your batting helmet in the Time Capsule at all times.

5) Feel free to purchase as many copies of this book as you like. It makes a wonderful gift—handsome and quietly impressive. It will be greatly appreciated by the most discerning and knowledgeable individuals and is suitable for any and all festive occasions—weddings, wakes, bar mitzvahs. In addition it is hand washable, comes in a pleasing array of gay decorator colors, and makes a pleasant and long lasting fire in case of fuel shortage.

6) Enjoy yourself. You deserve it.

Fondly,
Your friends, the authors

Contents

Where Have You Gone, VINCE DiMaggio?

SOME REFLECTIONS ON A BASEBALL CARD CHILDHOOD

Wayne Belardi, Ernie Fazio, Danny Napoleon
Jonas Salk, Gerry Vorhees, Sygman Ree
Elmer Singleton, Steve Souchak, Dan Osinski
Hailee Loakie, Caryl Chessman, Trig Vee Lee

On Monday morning July 27, 1953, at approximately 6:37 Greenwich Mean Time in the small coastal village of Panmunjom, Republic of North Korea, two smiling but not terribly cordial military attachés met to exchange copies of a truce agreement, a voluminous and hastily arranged cease-fire which would put an official end to their enmity.

World War 2.4 had finally ended. There was peace in the valley once more.

The immediate effects of this arch and copiously detailed military détente were many, some of a markedly portentous nature, others not. Only two were of any really permanent significance however to the vast sweeping vistas of human history. First, and most important, it marked the end of the first (or less traumatic) era of mankind's presence here on earth. Second (and this will be of interest only to you followers of the broader, less specific flow of western civilization), it enabled Theodore Samuel Williams to return to the starting lineup of the Boston Red Sox.

Farewell Ice Age. Stone Age. Dinosaurs. So long Creation. Fall. Redemption. Hello Gardol. Mr. Bluster. Plastic raincoats. Shake hands with Archie Bliar and Milton De Lugg. The era of the Hula-Hoop is upon us. Mr. Boynton and Herbert Philbrick presiding. Polio is down for the eight count. As are Mike DeJohn and Nino Valdez. Julius LaRosa now belongs to the ages. Along with arrowheads, dropsy, and the wireless. All tucked into our Plasticene memory books. To be pressed between the pages like mums. The Mouseketeers and Dody Goodman bless us. Dave Beck and Conway Twitty keep the rolls. Uncle Joe and Dwight the blessed monitor. With some help from Roy Cohn and Dick Clark.

And what of me with my Ozzie and Harriet briefcase? With my bottle of Slickum and my Pinky Lee hat? Where was I while Pupi Campo was blossoming? While Fats Domino was taking over the world?

Well, then it was in the bosom of this torpor, at the very height of its malignant menacing dormancy, that what I have piquantly come to think of as my youth unfolded in its sweet sleep of reason, like a fillip of moist vanilla nougat, in the family-sized Skybar of Life.

Wes Westrum, Paul Minner, Johnny Mize
Warren Hull, Tenley Albright, King Farouk
Paul Casanova, Jackie Brandt, Ralph Terry
Johnny Adie, Orval Faubus, Robin Luke

Why?

Because we like you.

M-O-U-S-E E E E E E E E E E E E E EEEEEEEEEEEEEEEEEEEEEEEEEEEEEE

We had our little indiscretions of course, our little lapses of manners and good taste. But for the most part our behavior was quite exemplary. Miss Frances wouldn't have it any other way. And what did I know, this warless war baby? This creature of the spreading middle affluence. What did I know, or even wish to know about anything? I knew exactly what Mr. Wizard told me. And what I read in the pages of "Children's Digest." Sitting in the third row of Sister Calamina's class, squeezing my hands together to make a sound like a fart. My mind was bordered on the north by Spin and Marty. And on the south by Gabby Hayes and Clarence Peaks. I had no idea who Georgi Malenkov was. Or why everybody loved Oveta Culp Hobby. Albert Anastasia meant nothing to me. Nor Guy Mollet nor Porfirio Rubirosa. I got up, went to school, did my homework. I ate a lot and took a bath every Saturday. I spit up whenever our class had a spelling bee. For all I knew the rest of the world was doing likewise. Bernard Goldfine slipped by all but unnoticed. Archbishop Makarios was just another pretty face. Dying popes, murdered princes, spectacular air wrecks. All existed just as double spreads in "Life." How did I know the fifties would ever end. How did I know the real world would catch up with us. I thought John Foster Dulles would rule us forever. It never occurred to me that Eddie **could** leave Debbie.

Rich Rich Rich in flavor. Smooth Smooth Smooth as silk.

More food energy than fresh whole milk.

Summer vacations. "My Little Margie." White Bucks. Jerry Lester. Flavor Straws. Danny and the Juniors.

Does it all seem like it never really happened?

Or that it took place in some murky static dream?

Abe Saperstein. Charcoal gray suits. Pink shirts. What's new in '52. Davy Crockett. Flat tops.

"Volare Ho Ho? Cantare Ho Ho Ho Ho!"

I think I slept through most of it anyway. I'll have to catch up with it sometime on the late show.

Charles Van Doren. DA's. Record hops. Snow coasters. Hurricane Carol. The Big Bopper.

"So long for a while. That's all the songs for a while.

"So long from your Hit Parade. And the tunes that you picked to be played.

"Sooooooooooooooooooooo long."

Estes Kefauver. Pierre Mendez-France. The sack dress. Randy Merriman. "Point of order." Spike heels.

4

All of it floating by me in a big latex bubble. Like a giant ball of regurgitated cat fur.

And only four sparks remaining in my memory—four images to root me to this epoch:

> 1) The sound of Don Pardo's booming voice.
> 2) The sight of Richard Costellano's sister naked.
> 3) The fear that Albert Dorish might beat me up.
> 4) And my three shopping bags full of baseball cards.

> Harry Malmberg, Eddie Joost, Johnny Hopp
> Willie Sutton, Chico Vejar, Keefe Brassel
> Glen Gorbus, Milo Candini, Tommy Hurd
> J. Fred Muggs, Gerry Mathers, Mar-vel-ous Vel

In the throes of my noxious preadolescence I cared very little for minor distinctions. So that the year was divided quite unredeemably for me into two separate air cells of time. There was school and vacation and none other. Vacation and school and that's all. We had all the regular seasons, of course, which brought interesting climactic variations, but the only thing that really held our attention was the slow steady erosion of the school year. There were 165 days in its tenure, plus time out for real and feigned illness. Our job was to make these disappear, or at least to pass in the least painful manner.

Fall was when the leaves fell and you had to go back to school.

Winter was when it was cold and snowy and you were still in school.

Spring was when it got warm again and you were still in school.

Summer was hot and sunny and lasted about fifteen minutes.

Then your vacation was mysteriously over. It was time to start over again.

Vacation was such a short period of time really that it had no further need of subdivision. It had a beginning and an end, but no middle. There wasn't enough time for a middle. It began in the third week of June and ended in the fourth week of June. We didn't lose it officially until September, but the death rattle began July Fourth. I started dreading the approach of Labor Day in April.

But schooltime was such a lengthy piece of work, such a tedious and overburdening experience, that it required further decompartmentalization—a little hacking up just to let us pass it down. It had to be broken up and attacked like a bacteria, lest it proliferate and overwhelm us completely. For this we invented a diversionary calendar. A series of milestones to exorcise the months. Our seasons were precisely gauged and measured. Our guiding points our five-and-dime minutiae.

September 6–October 1 FOOTBALL CARDS—The traditional beginning to the season. We were not terribly interested in football as it happened, involving as it did cold

5

weather and violence. So the cards quickly gave way to others on various subjects that were more in our line. Like television shows and fighter planes and singing groups. Racing cars and movie stars and locomotives. Joke cards, Historical cards. Davy Crockett cards. Cards that shimmered. Cards that glowed. Cards that changed colors. Cards that when rubbed revealed wondrous information. Cards that just sat there and looked up at you blankly. All for packing up in endless stacks of shoe boxes and storing under the eaves in dusty attics.

October 1–October 15 JACKKNIVES—For carving your initials into trees. For sticking into the ground before it froze.

October 15–October 31 PUNK—Long slender cork and bamboo tapers. You lit them and sat around and watched them smoke. God knows why. They smelled like chemically treated asparagus and tasted like soft moldering cardboard.

November 1–Thanksgiving YO-YOS—Cheerio. Duncan. Diamond-centered. Sleeping string. Around the world. Walk the doggie.

Thanksgiving–Christmas WATER PISTOLS—Shaped like rocket ships and little footballs and German lugers. Used right up until the winter froze the works.

Christmas–January 15 CAPS—In pistols. In cannisters. In old tomato cans. In the noses of plastic spaceships which exploded.

January 15–February 1 PUZZLES—Alphabetical puzzles, number puzzles, calendar puzzles. Puzzles that involved fitting BBs into clown's eyes.

February 1–February 15 PEZ—Foul-tasting sugar candy cubes. Shot into your mouth with a Pez gun. God knows why.

February 15–March 1 BUBBLE STUFF—Concentrated soapsuds in glass jars. Blown through a little plastic stick ring. Mostly for girls and more artistic types. Also good for little brothers and sisters.

March 1–March 15 KITES—Because March is coming in like a lion.

March 15–March 30 WOODEN AIRPLANES—Because now it's going out like a lamb.

April 1 ———— BASEBALL CARDS—Sure sign that the end is now in sight. The long agony of winter is almost over. The air softens and the backyard grows muddy. The last snow patches glisten and fade away.

Dick Gernert, Paul LaPalme, Ray Scarborough,
Jimmy Dodds, Specs O'Keefe, Madame Chiang,
Saul Rogovin, Mike Hershberger, Dave Hillman,
Althea Gibson, Gino Prado, C. K. Yang.

We bought our treasures in little dime stores called spas. Corner stores that were never on corners. Variety stores completely lacking in variety. They were generally owned by middle-aged men with psoriasis—paunchy citizens with sallow complexions and sour outlooks, who wore plaid woolen shirts no matter how hot it was and little felt hats that had repeatedly been stepped on. Their wives usually hung around in the background, squeezing the bread and keeping their eyes on the cash register. They wore white socks and babushkas and fashion glasses and always asked after the health of your dead aunt. The stores were called Pete's or Mike's or Al's or Joe's or Barney's. Or sometimes Frederick's if the owner was inclined to be formal. Or Bill and Mary's if the couple was happily married. Catchy names that reflected their vibrant characters. In my neighborhood there were two dozen of these establishments, scratching lustily against each other for survival. There was Connie's Spa which was owned by a paraplegic named Connie. And Harry's Deli which carried an incomplete selection of cold cuts. There was John's Market which had a wall of dirty magazines. And Tommy's Superette, which was quite a bit short of super. There was also B & J's, which didn't seem to stand for anything. And Lorenzo's which had sawdust on the floor. And Flannery's which had a stuffed codfish in the window. And Billy's Buy-Rite which sold Robitussin to winos. The one that we went to was called Eddie's. Eddie's Superteria or Eddie's Friendly Lunch—depending on Eddie's mood of the moment. It was operated by a huge Lithuanian guy named Eddie who had halitosis and was decidedly unfriendly.

Eddie sold everything from his storefront. You name it and Eddie was sure to have it—corn flakes, mustard plaster, snow tires, chili powder, teething rings, egg cups, garter belts, Nutty Putty, insecticide, light bulbs, gefilte fish, Scrabble sets. If you were interested in a deal on a forklift there was a good chance that Eddie could help you out. He even carried little packages of dehydrated night crawlers on the chance that a stray fisherman might wander in. And all of this from just six hundred square feet of floor space—a good part of which was taken up by Mrs. Eddie (a massive woman who wore overalls and hip boots and carried what looked to be a zip gun in her budge). He had a fruit stand and a vegetable bin and a bakery counter. And the world's largest supply of canned olives. He had a pinball machine and a Coke machine and a coffee machine. And greeting cards and an ice cream freezer and a grab bag. He had hundreds of cans of mushroom lentil soup and a whole aisleful of marinated chick-peas. He had pickled pigs' feet in big jars the size of bass drums and more rhubarb pie filling than you would have thought humanly possible. If there was anything that nobody could possibly be interested in, Eddie was sure to have laid in a big supply. Fifty-pound polyethylene bags of popping corn, giant jars of green and blue Maraschino cherries, felt pennants of uninteresting historical monuments, boxes of faded monogrammed party hats and favors. He had a giant cutout of the Philip Morris midget and the largest display of sanitary napkins in the East. He kept a sale bin full of dented cans of cat food and always featured Ovaltine at 6 cents off. There was also a wall completely lined with novelty items, all mounted and neatly arranged on cardboard cards. Plastic change purses, colored rabbits' feet, copper key rings, laminated belt buckles, Confederate flags, silver nail files. Enough sewing needles to supply an army of seamstresses. More Popeye rub-ons than he could sell in fifty years. And for his customers with intellectual inclinations — the latest issues of "Argosy" and "Motor Trend." All suspended from metal clips on filigreed wires. All surrounded by paperback westerns with no covers.

But it was the candy counter that was really the center of interest, the one area that held our undivided attention. It was here that Eddie spent most of his time, although I'm sure he would have preferred it otherwise. You could spend fifteen minutes here with just a nickel, trying to decide whether to buy one old-fashioned or two. You could change your mind back and forth a dozen times or more, driving Eddie right to the brink of a nervous breakdown.

"Look, I have to wait on Mrs. Bonaturo now. Hurry up, will you, with your 8 cents' worth of crap. You kids are driving me absolutely crazy. And put that comic book down, this isn't a goddamn library."

Malted milk balls, Mary Janes, Red Hot Dollars — Fire Balls, root beer barrels, jelly beans — sugar cones, tar babies, orange slices — nonpareils, goober peanuts, wintergreens — Canada Mints, Jujubes, wax moustaches — sour balls, licorice whips, marshmallow bananas. Everything a human being could possibly wish for. Everything a Lincoln penny could possibly buy.

And baseball cards. Baseball cards. Baseball cards.

Nippy Jones, Willard Marshall, Connie Ryan
Burr Tillstrom, Grace Metalious, James Dean
Charlie Keller, Billy Hitchcock, Stu Miller
Doris Duke, Maurice Podoloff, Fulton J. Sheen

They appeared sometime during the first weeks of March when the world was beginning to thaw out around us. News of spring training was slowly drifting northward and our surviving another school year now seemed possible. Oh, they were beautiful and reassuring to behold, brand new and glistening crisply in their packages. Packed into cardboard cartons of 24 and 120, stuck behind glassed partitions and stacked on counters. An indication that the world was still in order, a promise of pleasant days and easeful nights. Bowman cards, Fleer cards, Topps cards — in green wrappers, blue wrappers, and red. And how the news spread quickly through the neighborhood — as at the coming of some inestimable personage. And we quickly down to the corner to check it out, to verify the new arrivals for ourselves. Yes, the pictures had changed a little bit. And the backs of the cards were altered oh so slightly. But they were still basically the same cards as before. There were some things even **they** couldn't change. And the joy of breaking open the year's first package. To see what Marty Marion was going to look like this year. To see if any of the old uniforms had been altered. To see if everyone was still as young as before. And the sweet pleasant smell of the bubble gum, and the sweet pleasant melting of it in your mouth.

8

And the secure feel of the cards in your pocket, and the knowledge that they were yours and yours alone. The prospect of all the packages to be opened, the thought of all the new cards to be flipped. The possibilities of wheeling and dealing and pyramiding. The notion that maybe the Red Sox **could** win the Pennant. And above it all their splendid physical presence. Their sturdiness. Their symmetry. Their artful grace. The way they looked all stacked up on your dresser. And the mysterious things we knew they really meant.

There was Bob Allison and Moe Berg and Joe Dobson. And Gary Bell and Don Blasingame and Zeke Bella. There was Johnny Blanchard, who was extremely overrated, and Buddy Blattner, whom nobody knew. There was Steve Boros and Marshall Bridges and Lou Brissie. And Tom Brewer, who was no relation to Jim. There were team cards and manager cards and rookie cards. And cards with all sorts of interesting statistics. There was Ernie Broglio and Bill Bruton and Pete Burnside. And Wally Burnette, who had gotten a huge bonus. There was Bud Byerly and Wayne Causey and Bob Chance. And John Buzhardt—whose **h** was strangely silent. There was a card for every player, or so they said, and as many ways to collect them as collectors.

There was the dabbler and the addict and the connoisseur. There was the compilator and the fan and the gambler.

The dabbler bought seldom, if ever. He really wasn't that interested in baseball.

The addict bought often and very heavily. He didn't particularly care what he got.

The connoisseur only bought what really interested him. He bought most of his cards from private parties.

The compilator thought of himself as an artist—a totality of scope his only ambition.

The fan preferred members of the home team. A rare card meant nothing to him.

Whereas the gambler was interested primarily in quantity. Making something out of nothing, or even less.

I was a gambler I'll have to admit it—with a slight touch of the compilator and the fan. I was a gambler because that was my nature. Only later did I turn into a fan.

There was Murry Dickson, who looked about fifty. And John Goryl, who looked about twelve. There was Phil Clark, who had very high cheekbones. And Dom DiMaggio, who had no cheekbones at all. There was Lou Limmer, who had a gap between his teeth. And Harry Elliott, who wore school-teacherish glasses. And Johnny Kucks, who looked a little like Johnny Pesky, and Nelson King, who looked a lot like Andy Gump. There was Ed Charles and Nelson Chittum and Sandy Consuegra. And Ray Crone and Bert Hamric and Sam Dente. There was an endless supply of pitchers named Miller. And an infinite number of infielders named Jones.

If you wanted to collect cards you needed some business sense. A firm foundation based on sound management principle. You needed to approach it like an administrative problem. Otherwise you definitely ran the risk of going under.

First you needed a well-established line of credit—which meant getting a nickel or dime from your mother. This was not always as easy as it sounded and so alternative channels of financing were recommended.

Second you needed a provision for capital expenditure—which involved a trip to Eddie's or Lorenzo's, or whatever. This was actually the most exciting part of the deal. Fraught with every imaginable purchasing variable.

Next you needed a proper inventory management—which included dividing your new purchases into categories. There were those cards which you were definitely going to keep, and those which were more or less expendable.

Finally you needed a way of progressing with your merchandise—of utilizing all the goods you had accumulated. Sales promotion. Investment credits. Material stockpiling. Making the most of your ornate pasteboard empire.

Like the paragons of junior capitalism that we were, we used all sorts of variations on these principles. Hedging and haggling and speculating. Taking advantage of every possible angle. We used our cards to make more cards and still more cards. Turning ourselves into veritable bubble gum entrepreneurs.

There was Art Ditmar and Harry Dorish and Arnold Earley. And Doc Edwards and Dee Fondy and Don Ferrarese. There was Del Crandall, who looked upright and law-abiding, and Jim Pisoni, who looked like a second-story man. There was Art Fowler and Joe Foy and Aubrey Gatewood. And George Alusik and Mudcat Grant and Tom Morgan. And Jim Turner, who had probably been **born** a pitching coach. And Dick Donovan, who lived right in the next town. There was Howie Goss and Bob Giggie and Don Gile. And Marv Grissom and Warren Hacker and Bob Hale. And of course Don Rudolph, who was married to a stripper. And Larry Jansen, who had ten or eleven kids.

Every day at three o'clock, beginning in April, I would appear down at Eddie's with my nickel. This was my reward for maintaining my good behavior—a little bribe to keep the authorities from our door. There was usually a line of kids down there long before me, buying pimple balls and magnetic Scottie dogs and etch-a-sketch sets. I had trouble maintaining my composure at this time, such were the pressures of pure avarice building inside me. Then the nickel into Eddie's calloused palm and my hands upon the blue and orange wrapper. The wax paper very quickly under my fingernails. The smell of the gum bursting up and into the air. The feel of the virgin cards very firm against my fingertips. The hope that something marvelous was lurking there inside. Eddie Haas, rookie star of '59? But I've already got him twenty-seven times. Bill Renna—who the hell is Bill Renna? And what does he have to grin about like that? And would you believe it, another Bob Trowbridge. They must put him in every other package. Connie Grob? Well, at least that's something new. Even if he is the worst pitcher on the Senators. Oh no, not Steve Gromek again. You can't even give that guy away. And I don't think I can stand another Joe Cunningham. That's the third time I've gotten him since Wednesday. One card that I didn't have before. One card for my nickel and my effort. Well, Connie Grob into the left pocket of my jacket, and then, later, into my Red Rooster shoe box. All the rest into the back pocket of my peg pants, to be stored in my green Stoppette carton. Some cards for

10

selling off to the rich kids, some cards for trading with adversaries and friends, some cards for keeping in my collection for the fun of it, but most cards just for matching and flipping. To see what they could turn themselves into, to see what sort of treasures they could bring. The gum neat and cracking into my mouth, and myself home in time for "Johnny Jupiter." Back up the springtime street as I had come. With the sun slowly sliding down our roof. To live another day without Sibbi Sisti. To see what all my tomorrows might possibly bring.

There was Fritz Brickell and Art Cecarelli and Johnny Groth. And Billy Harrell and Jack Harshman and Ray Herbert. Frank Baumholtz, who was always being sent down. Gair Allie, who was always being brought up. Charley Bishop. Chico Fernandez and Harry Perkowski. Billy O'Dell, Dutch Leonard and Memo Luna. Jerry Davie who was perennially promising. Johnny Briggs who would always disappoint. The Milwaukee Braves with their ball boys, Wick and Blossfield. The Detroit Tigers with their bat boys, O'Brien and Kelly. Bill Virdon, who looked like a sociology professor. Bob Skinner, who looked like a counterman at Nedicks.

What I did with my cards was I flipped them. In a desperate effort to make their numbers increase. I joined in games of chance with my fellow collectors. No quarter asked and none ever given.

How this worked was disarmingly simple (deceptively simple to the innocently uninitiated):

You drew a line in the dust or on the pavement and flipped your cards from this line toward a wall. Each player scaling his own card in turn, the winner of the previous round going last. The card closest to the wall won the pot. No leaners or doctored cards allowed. I spent 60 percent of my youth in this practice. Drilling daily and searching diligently for pigeons. Bent over cracked asphalt driveways in total silence. Scaling slivers of colored cardboard toward old garages. And I was moderately successful at it also. Amassing three shopping bags full of cards. Not a particularly creative way to spend a boyhood. But not a completely misspent youth, it seems to me. Wafting cards out across shadowy schoolyards. Seeing them float and settle softly to the ground. The hours gently rolling by until sunset. Like the fifties rolling gently through our minds. The happiness of having your card inch out another's. The agony of losing a lucky Billy Pleis. The joy of watching your stack of cards increasing. The knowledge that your youth would never end. Eighteen Lou Kretlows. Twenty-one Frank Malzones. A stack of Johnny Logans as thick as a Snickers. More Garry Roggenburks than the mind could comprehend. And over it all the sweet smile of Spring Byington. Assuring us that nothing could possibly go wrong.

Of course there were other things that you could do with your baseball cards. And other people in their various ways managed to do them. How you utilized them depended on your temperament. The possibilities for variation were practically limitless. You could play games with them on rainy afternoons, using the pictures as surrogate ballplayers. You could arrange and rearrange them in various categories and make lists of all your multiple arrangements. By position, by team, by batting average. By number, by achievement, by personal preference. You could invent various individual rating systems, make trades, construct dream teams, determine strategy. You could pile them up on your bed when you had a cold and give each and every one of them a good talking to. You could paste them on walls or on mirrors, or in scrapbooks with little plastic windows. You could mail them away to be autographed by the players, or you could sell them to an acquisitive collector. You might even have been able to eat them, although I never knew anyone who did. I didn't go in much for any of these variations. I was more interested in out and out pyramiding. I liked to gamble and take risks with my baseball cards. I liked to see what kind of booty they could bring.

There was Ted Lepcio and Don Lock and Art Mahaffey. And Lucky Lohrke and Morrie Martin and Nelson Mathews. There was Dave Hoskins not looking particularly hopeful. And Willard Nixon not looking hopeful at all. There were umpire cards and coach cards and World Series cards. And cards of Warren Giles and Ford Frick and William Harridge. There was Ted Williams in the cockpit of a fighter. And Stan Musial giving a Little Leaguer advice. There was Lou Gehrig saying farewell in the Stadium. And Casey Stengel gagging it up with Bob Cerv. There was Buster Narum and Julio Navarro and Ray Ripplemeyer. And Don Nottebart and John Orsino and Bobo Osborne. And there was even a card of Wee Willie Keeler, although none of us knew exactly who he was.

You didn't have to play baseball to collect baseball cards. You didn't even have to be a fan, it often seemed. Although most of us rooted patiently for the Red Sox. And played pickup games the whole summer long, getting up at ungodly hours in the morning, trudging down to grassless playgrounds after dawn, playing unceasingly hour after hour; from sunup to sundown, and sometimes longer. The heat shimmering like a shock wave over the infield. The dust settling down into our lungs. Salt and sweat covering our brown necks and forearms. Our hands calloused and stinging from untaped bats. And then home again when it finally became hopeless. With the ball just a pale shadow against the night. To sit on the porch or in the backyard with the crickets. To listen to our beloved home team lose again — Norm Zauchin, Billy Goodman, Sammy White, Frank Sullivan, Mel Parnell, Ike Delock. Was there ever such a monument to futility? Was there anything that could disappoint us more? Murray Wall, Milt Bolling, Sam Mele — Karl Olson, Del Wilbur, Sid Hudson. If you haven't rooted for such a ball team you know nothing. You are innocent of the true meaning of human suffering. The only constant of my boyhood was the Red Sox — and the uninspired mediocrity of their play. That and the reassuring presence of my baseball cards: flipping back and forth through the slow summer days.

There was Stubby Overmire and Whitey Ford and Bob Porterfield. And Eddie Pellagrini who hit a home run his first time up. And Jerry Priddy and Ken Raffensberger and Bob Ramazotti. And Hal Reniff, although he might have come a bit later. And Jay Ritchie and Preacher Roe and Andre Rodgers. And Ray Scarborough and Barney Schultz and Billy Short. There was Rip Sewall who threw a pitch called the blooper ball. And Rollie Sheldon who threw pitches you couldn't name. There was Roy Smalley and Russ Snyder and Jack Spring. And Ebba St. Claire, whose name evoked strange images. There was Bob Speake and Stuffy Stirnweiss and Pete Suder. And Don Zimmer whose name evoked nothing at all.

It is true, of course, that nothing remains totally stationary; that even the baseball cards were not an absolute constant. They changed their style very subtly through the years, although the changes were more real to us than apparent. Sometimes the players were pictured on them horizontally—sometimes they came at you straight up and down. Some years there were action pictures in the background. Some years just a head and shoulder shot. There were drawings in 1948, mostly profiles in '49 and '50. Sometimes there were reproductions of autographs on the cards; sometimes just printed or typewritten letters. And the backs of the cards varied also, in makeup and information provided. There were cartoon players' biographies some years, with capsulated major league records. Or there were one-paragraph histories of the players, with a year-by-year list of their achievements. There were quizzes and little puzzles for you to solve. "What's a pitchout?" "What does 'banjo hitter' mean?" There were blanks that you rubbed for magic answers. And always the long lists of vital statistics. The graphics and artwork got gradually better. After a while you could make out Wes Stock's face. The years went by, but I didn't see them going. The cards got better and baseball got much worse. The fifties disappeared from my memory like a daydream. I got older although I'll be damned if I know how.

There was Larry Jackson and Sheldon Jones and Leo Kiely. And Jerry Kendall and Thornton Kipper and Howie Koplitz. There was Bob Elliott, who was known as Mr. Team, and Russ Nixon, who was the Chocolate Malted Kid. There was Walt Masterson and Danny McDevitt and Phil Masi. And Rudy Minarcin and Paul Minner and Billy Moran. There was Lenny Green who wasn't good, but who tried hard. And Willie Kirkland who was good, but wouldn't bother. There was Billy Rohr, who had a one-hitter as a rookie, and Dom Zanni, who really couldn't pitch at all. There was Joe Ostrowski and Max Alvis and Jim King—and Leo Posada and Marino Pieretti and Frank Funk. And Bud Podbielan, who looked a bit like death warmed over. And George Zuverink, who looked like death without the warmth.

And then one year it was all suddenly over. Mousecartoontime had finally run its course. Somehow baseball did not seem so important to us anymore. And neither, of course, did the collecting of its cards. Dick Tomanek and Bob Grim had retired. Duke Snider was very much an old man. José Melis and Frank Parker were gone forever. Snooky Lanson and his crowd had disappeared. It was 1959, almost the end of the decade. The year that Harvey Kuenn won the American League batting championship. The year that Frankie Avalon made his hit record of "Venus." The year Pat Boone composed "Twixt Twelve and Twenty." That was the year we all discovered sophistication. The year we began to put our baseball cards away.

It started out slowly enough, almost surreptitiously. Like a virus growing quietly in your blood. We had expected it, although we were not really prepared for it. It all seemed to have come on us much too soon. Our indifference was not a sudden thing after all. The habits of years are not that easily discontinued. It needed time to be absorbed by our systems. Like a best friend who suddenly moves away. But still it was there, there was no use denying it. Like the final reel of the Saturday morning serial. You could ignore it, but that wouldn't make it easier. The signs of our growing up were too readily apparent. Nobody in the neighborhood seemed interested in the new cards. Nobody played with their Erector sets anymore. Nobody played stickball against the bleachers in the town field. Nobody made walkie-talkies out of orange juice cans. We were all looking forward anxiously to high school, to record hops and class rings and making out. Nobody wanted to match pennies for Rocky Nelson. Everybody seemed to have more important things to do.

And so the cards stayed in the glass cases in Eddie's. And our nickels went for less childish things. I myself was saving up for a motor boat. The fifties sank into my consciousness like a stone. Red Buttons and Russell Arms faded from memory. Uncle Toonoose and Corporal Rusty floated away. Bobo Olson outgrew the middleweight division. George Fenneman no longer kept the secret word. And long afternoons of flipping baseball cards left us forever. Long evenings of counting our winnings disappeared. And after a while I no longer opened my shoe boxes. And soon afterward my mother put them away for good. And the surprising thing was that I never really missed them. Or even thought of them in any special way. And very gradually the memory of all of it faded. And just became another thing we used to do.

Ted Wilks, Freddy Green, Gordy Coleman
Ethyl Mertz, Silky Sullivan, Sonny Fox
Milt Graff, Walt Moryn, Brooks Lawrence
Jack Lascoolie, Bridey Murphy, Wally Cox

And that is the way you always lose your childhood.
And that is what this book is all about.

This Kid Is Going
to Make It

Someone once asked Al Ferrara of the Dodgers why he wanted to be a baseball player. He said because he always wanted to see his picture on a bubble gum card. Well, me too. It's an ego trip.
— Jim Bouton, "Ball Four."

And a happy landing on a chocolate bar.
— Shirley Temple,
"The Good Ship Lollipop."

Once upon a time (and a very good time it was, too) when dinosaurs still roamed the earth, and Don McNeil still marched around the breakfast table — long before Red Buttons had become a tragedian — even before Don Ameche had invented the telephone — there was a place known as Brooklyn, New York, where a team known as the Dodgers played a game known as baseball. Brooklyn was the birthplace of Chester A. Riley, the urban Middletown of Gino Prado and Ralph J. Cramden. And the Dodgers were its Beloved Bumbling Bums, the team that Dana Andrews used to bamboozle Richard Loo. Baseball of course needs little introduction — it's the one with the glove and the moustache. Muntz made radios and Flako made pie curst. De Soto made automobiles and so did Kaiser-Fraiser. And Topps made baseball cards and almost everybody bought them. Even diminutive and bespectacled class creeps who couldn't tell Harry Malmberg from Marion Motley.

Of course there is no such place as Brooklyn anymore. It has been cemented over and converted into a parking lot. The streets of Flatbush are awash with neon blight. The hills of Williamsburg are rotted through with highrise pestilence. And there is no such team as the Dodgers anymore, either. Since Walter O'Malley packed their bags for California, the vacuous land of Ralph Williams has engulfed them, their only memorial a stack of Chili Taco Burgers. Even baseball seems to have pulled a disappearing act, becoming just a further extension of the shoddy world of show business.

There are two hundred and fifty teams in the major leagues now.

All the players look like William Morris agents.

Nothing in fact seems to be as it once was — when Omar Bradley and Molly Goldberg ran the world.

Nothing that is except the Topps Chewing Gum Company, which still persists in acting out our childhood fantasies. Still producing pasteboard trading cards of our sporting heroes. Still exchanging signet rings for Bazooka comics. And still very much on Brando's Brooklyn waterfront, as if nothing about our world had ever changed.

And so the other day, out of respect for this persistent phenomenon, I took myself over to Topps for a little social call. A minor genuflection in the direction of the fifties, a tip of the Hatlo Hat to Rootie Kazootie and Polka Dottie. I hiked up my peg pants and slipped on my penny loafers, and packed a fluffer-nutter into my Roy Rogers lunch pail. And off I went on my red Flexible Flyer, across the years that just never would wait up. Under the boardwalk and out over the mountain. In search of my youth or a reasonable facsimile. To prove once again that not just the dead know Brooklyn. And that it isn't true that you can't go home again.

Topps Chewing Gum, Inc., of Brooklyn, New York, and Duryea, Pennsylvania, is the largest manufacturer of bubble gum and bubble gum–related novelty items in the world. Last year the company sold over one and a half billion pieces of Bazooka, its penny piece of bubble gum; manufactured over 500 million sports and other collector cards; and had revenues of $33.8 million, gross profit on sales of $12.9 million, and net income before taxes of $2.5 million. Now this is a hell of a lot of bubble gum no matter how you happen to look at it, and it is managing to make a lot of people quite rich, in its calm and quiet bubble-gumish manner. In fact, last year, when Topps made its first public stock offering (the corporate equivalent of trading a wilted Tommy Henrich and a torn Harry Dorish for two Kenny Keltners and a box of pop-it beads) at $17.50 a share (since risen to $23), the prospectus issued in this regard by the prestigious New York banking firm of White, Weld and Co. went to great pains to point out to potential investors, in as casual and deadpan a manner as they could summon, that Topps' president, Joel Shorin, had been reimbursed for his services in 1971 to the tune of $114,363, not including profit-sharing and stock options. A hundred big ones for the Brooklyn Bazooka Baron. Twice the salary of the secretary of state. The company's other key executives: Abram Shorin, chairman; Philip B. Shorin, executive vice president; Edward E. Shorin, vice president international; Arthur T. Shorin, vice president marketing, were paid an average of $84,000 apiece, not including profit-sharing and stock options, during this period.

All those nickels seem to mount up pretty fast. Bubble gum isn't just peanuts after all.

Topps lists among the products it has sold: Shazam, Jeepers Creepers, Sweet Sippy, Flying Things, Love Initials, Groovy Stickons, Snappy 'Gator, Bozo, Bazooklets, Gold Rush, Big Tooth, Big Buddy, Bubblegum Shake and Big Mouth on a Stick. Snappy 'Gator is a small plastic alligator's head filled with bubble gum. Big Tooth is a large plastic molar filled with bubble gum. Big Buddy is a foot-long ruler-shaped wad of bubble gum. And Big Mouth on a Stick is more or less self-explanatory. Topps sells its products in 55 foreign countries, has licensed manufacturers in 10 other countries, has its Bazooka Joe trademark registered in 130 countries, distributes its products through a network of 5,000 regional wholesalers, and sells raw materials, confectionary products, and countless thousands of tons of bubble gum to independent candy manufacturers and retail confectionary outlets throughout the United States, South America, western Europe, and every other reasonably accessible nook and cranny of what we have laughingly come to refer to as Civilization.

The mind does not just boggle. It rolls over on its back and has spasms.

The company that calls its location the bubble gum capital of the world has its main offices in the Bush Terminal section of Brooklyn, a waterfront locale not particularly noted for decorous gentility. It is an area of deserted piers and grimy truck stops, of sulfurous air and rasping foghorns—the sort of place a self-respecting sea gull might avoid, the kind of spot even Joey Gallo might have found unnerving. Tanker trucks rumble steadily down its streets. The harbor wind whips unrelentingly along its sidewalks. It is nowhere near the ghost of Ebbetts Field. The spirits of Carl Erskine and Billy Cox are not encountered.

Topps' headquarters at 254 Thirty-sixth Street is in a remodeled and startlingly whitewashed six-story warehouse. The building itself resembles a goiterous vanilla torte that someone has laid open with the dull edge of a spatula. It is surrounded by truck terminals and cold storage outlets and by buildings that look like refugees from Rikers Island. Eddie the Pastrami King lies just across the block, advertising the best all-purpose grinders in New York City. The alleyways between the warehouses are paved with cobblestones. Frozen orange rinds and speckled eggshells line the cracks. Topps has the entire second floor of its building. Uneeda Doll Company and Gibraltar Fabrics above and below. The office of the sports director is just off the vestibule, a wooden cubicle enclosed with ice-blue clouded glass.

> Owen was inducted into the Army at the end of the 1950 season in which he batted .237 in 119 games. Drove in 50 runs. Joined the Browns in the closing days of the 1949 season, appearing in 2 games. Began in organized baseball with Newark of the Ohio State League in 1944. Saw action with 7 different teams. These included Memphis, Raleigh, Elmira, Springfield.
> — From the 1951 baseball card of Owen Friend, second baseman, St. Louis Browns.

Sy Berger is on a water diet.

"I drink fourteen or fifteen glasses of the stuff every day. And you know I'm getting

19

so I actually like it."

He keeps a pitcher of ice water on his desk, right next to a display pack of Bazooka. Each visitor is offered a sample snoot. He seems a bit miffed when most of them decline. He pours himself a stiff one now and leans back in his black Barcalounger.

"I've lost about thirty-five pounds in a little less than four months. I feel like a million dollars. Reggie Jackson called me from the Coast this morning to complain about the stereo set we sent him. Says the terminals aren't hooked up or some damn thing. I said to him—'You guys can't worry me anymore, Reggie—I'm thin. I'm a thin person now.' Believe me, I feel like a kid again, like at least a quarter of a million dollars."

He smiles sheepishly, having reduced his earlier estimate.

"A great kid though, Reggie. A great ballplayer and a heck of a nice guy."

Seymour Berger, head of Topps Chewing Gum Sports Department, surrogate grandfather to baseball's great and would-be great, and the unquestioned baseball card king of the Universe, grins broadly at the memory of this encounter. He is proud of the exploits of his kids. Even if they do like to act up on occasion. And he really does look like a million dollars too, in his twill suit and regimental tie. As is befitting a man of his position—a man responsible for the baseball cards of the nation. In excess of two hundred and fifty million of them last year, worth a cool $8 million retail. Plus a like number of football, basketball, and hockey cards. Sold with 25 million slabs of pink bubble gum. Not precisely a graying Johnny Bench perhaps, but a considerably svelter version of Durocher. A living testament to the wonders of Irwin Stillman.

"It's funny how things have a way of growing on you, you know. No matter what business you happen to be in. I remember when we first started out here almost twenty-five years ago. We had nothing. Just an idea and a list of players' names. I was the assistant sales manager and the head of the Sports Department, too. I used to write all the copy for the baseball cards myself, in my living room, at home on the weekends. Jesus, it was murder. You don't know the agony of trying to think up something nice to say about some guy who hit .176 last year and made 25 errors. What can you say—'This guy stinks'?"

He shakes his head mournfully at the recollection.

"And our competition had it all over us too. They were very firmly entrenched. They had all the really big stars locked up and all the major areas of distribution. It was tough. I remember once we got an order for two dozen cartons of cards from a big discount chain somewhere in the Middle West and we practically went through the roof with exaltation. We walked around in a daze for a week. Now look at all this."

His neatly manicured hand sweeps quickly over the landscape. The spacious rooms that comprise the executive offices, the billiard room paneling, the casually elegant Scandinavian furniture. A feeling of prosperity hangs in the air like a dust cloud.

"In the beginning we intended to sign up every minor leaguer no matter how lousy he was. That wasn't too workable, though, so we had to become more selective. Then we got a former major league scout—Turk Karam—a really grand guy who used to work in the Dodgers organization, and we sent him down to all the minor league camps and the rookie instructional leagues and told him to sign up only legitimate prospects, to sort of separate the wheat from the chaff. And he did this for a number of years; did a great job too, I might say, in addition—I'm not saying every guy we signed up made it to the majors, but none of the guys we let go ever worked out. Anyhow, we would give the player a one dollar bill as a binder. But after a while guys were starting to complain. What the hell can I do with a buck, they'd say. And they were right of course. So we raised it to five dollars. Which is what it is today. Steak money we call it, that's steak with an "eak." Then one year there was this very ordinary looking shortstop in the Dodger organization—somewhere in the very low minors—a real scrawny kid, nothing memorable about him at all. And everybody says—this kid will never make it. He can't hit. He's too small. Got bad hands. A weak arm. Forget about him. The guys in his own organization said this. And so we didn't sign him, and of course it was Maury Wills."

He pauses briefly to let the weight of this sink in.

"Well, Maury stayed angry at us for quite some time after that, as you can well imagine, even after he made it to the majors. He didn't sign up with us until about his eighth year with the Dodgers. He was the only major leaguer we didn't have under contract. You couldn't blame him of course. So after that we went back to signing everybody in the minors. That way we don't make any headaches for ourselves."

There do not appear to be too many headaches of any variety for Topps these days. Even Marvin Miller's name evokes only a patient grimace. The Baseball Players' Association negotiated a new contract with Topps in 1968 with card royalties adjusted sharply upward.

"No, we don't have any real problems with anyone. Because we treat everybody we do business with fairly. Oh, occasionally we'll have a little trouble with some kid. But it's usually straightened out within a couple of days. You see, it really isn't to a player's advantage to hold out on us. What's the point? He has nothing to gain and everything to lose. We pay a guy $250 when he makes a major league roster. And $250 a year each year he stays up. Plus we have a royalty agreement worked out on a percentage basis that guarantees the players a certain cut of our profit. This year each guy will end up with about $400. Plus we pay him even if he gets sent down during the year, provided we use his picture, of course, or he has been with the club the first 30 days of the season. And each player gets the same amount of money. Or, if he wants, he can pick out a special premium from this catalogue of merchandise we have made up. We get this stuff wholesale from RCA and General Electric. It's got everything in it but replacement pitching arms."

He hands a stamp redemptionlike booklet across the desk to me. It is full of pictures of pastel patio furniture and color televisions.

"Richie Allen took a new refrigerator this year. You know one of those deals that crushes ice and shines your shoes. Some of the guys let their royalties accumulate.

Dick Green bought some farm machinery with his. And Al Kaline just bought his kid a new car. So you see it's really a good deal all around. Are you sure I couldn't interest you in some ice water?"

Topps has been around for thirty-five years now. It had its antecedents in the American Leaf Tobacco Company, a jobber and importer of tobacco for independent cigar manufacturers, founded in 1890 by Morris Shorin, the grandfather of the present Topps president.

American Leaf was a moderately successful company in its field and its owners enjoyed a certain prosperity. But the Depression of the thirties hit it hard and burgeoning automation hit it harder. The need for diversification quickly became apparent. So the Shorin brothers — Abram, Ira, Philip and Joseph — began searching around for a secure and profitable sideline. They decided they wanted to sell a product that was consumed and could have brand identification. They thought at first of going into the produce business. But the specter of frigid dawns and icy marketplaces quickly put an end to this particular line of thinking. They finally settled on chewing gum manufacture, for reasons both fiscal and sentimental. It was a product with strong consumer appeal, was easily identifiable and readily marketable, it made use of their existing channels of distribution and was not overcrowded with small pockets of competition. It also did not require a large initial investment, and held the promise of being a little fun in the bargain. The first gum was produced in 1938, a one cent fruit-flavored cube which became popular as a change-maker for small variety stores. The name Topps was chosen for obvious reasons. The company's slogan during the course of World War II — a motto that they have chosen inexplicably to perpetuate — was "Don't Talk Chum. Chew Topps Gum" — a cloying variation on the "slip lip, sink ship" theme that might have proved embarrassing even to Irving Berlin. The first bubble gum product was introduced shortly after the end of the war — a 5 cent bar of gum called Bazooka. This was followed by the familiar pink penny piece, with accompanying comic fortune and premium offer. The other novelty items followed inevitably and more or less inexorably.

But it was in 1951 that Topps really hit the confectionary jackpot. That was the year that they reinvented the baseball card, thus insuring their niche in American boyhood immortality. Other companies had produced sporting cards before them — Bowman, and Goudey Gum, most notably — but none with such all-encompassing voracity, or with anything approaching Topps' brand of evangelical dynamism. Topps was a relatively small company, lacking in experience and the means of national distribution, but once committed to a product they remained committed. And they were totally committed to the notion of baseball cards. They were fighting very strongly entrenched competition, companies with all the players and the markets sewn up. But they have never been particularly noted for their timidity, nor were they noticeably backward when it comes to promotion.

So should you be interested in buying some baseball cards these days, you are going to have to do your business with Topps. They are the only ones around who still make them. They have committed their competition to the ground.

"We had everything down here until 1965—everything—the bubble gum-making machinery, the card-printing apparatus, everything. We had 8 different offices, and warehouses in about 5 different buildings in the neighborhood. It was ridiculous. It took you a week to get anything done. So seven years ago we moved all the plant and storage facilities to Duryea, Pennsylvania. To a big modern plant with 400,000 square feet of floor space. We have 1,000 people working there now—turning out bubble gum and sports cards and all our different novelty products. And we have 150 people still working here in Brooklyn—the executive and editorial branch of the thing."

There is a picture of the new Duryea plant on the wall, looking like a mile-and-a-half-long serrated egg crate.

"We bring in all the ingredients in tank trucks and railroad cars and store them in custom-designed silos and bins. All the mixing and blending is done automatically—with huge consoles and preset weighing systems. The gum is then taken to the seasoning room where the flavorings are added to the base. The basic ingredients are sugar, dextrose, and corn syrup. After that it gets pushed and pulled through our specialized forming machinery, cut and circled with a Bazooka comic, or shaped into various novelty items and then wrapped and sent to the shipping department. The whole operation takes just a couple of hours. But we are extremely careful about every single step. We have 118 steps of manufacture and 23 separate quality checks. We take great pride in the quality of our bubble gum."

He says this like a man who really means it. A man devoted to Snappy 'Gator and Big Buddy. There is a new product on his desk this very minute—a caramel version of Big Mouth on a Stick. He tosses it underhand into the folds of his briefcase, for display later at an afternoon sales conference.

"The making of the baseball cards is another matter entirely. That is a fairly complicated process, what with all the specialized printing and photography. But basically we do it by the lithography method—after the cards have been pasted up in the Art Department. We put them on square cardboard sheets—132 cards to each sheet—the backs and the fronts on the same piece of cardboard. Then the sheets are cut and collated and sorted by a special machine that we invented and patented ourselves, so that each series receives a proper mixture. These are the two hardest things we have to deal with in producing baseball cards—getting the color photography just right and making sure the cards are mixed and sorted properly. A lot of kids complain that they keep getting the same cards over and over. This is the biggest problem we have with the cards. But actually it has nothing to do with us at all. We print up the same number of cards for each player—stars and unknown rookies alike. And we distribute them evenly throughout the country. But because we print the cards in series—six series, six weeks apart—we sometimes run into backups at the distribution point. Say a guy with a small corner store in the Bronx will order twenty cartons of Series One cards. He sells out in three or four weeks and so he reorders fifteen cartons. By now the kids in his area have all the Series One cards, so that by the time Series Two is ready for distribution, the guy finds himself with ten cartons of Series One left over. So he goes light on Series Two, all the time trying to get rid of his Series One. By the time the fifth or sixth series has come out, he has himself backlogged right up to his eyeballs. It's sort of a snowball effect in reverse. It's a real problem for us and always has been, and it's really hard to know exactly what to do about it."

He looks discouraged for a moment, although hardly despondent. This is clearly a touchy problem with Topps. All those Charley Browns and so few Joe Shlabotnicks. And the baseball season growing longer all the time.

"As far as designing and producing the cards goes, that process begins right after the World Series. We all get together and sit down in a big room and begin going over the prospective rosters of each team. Trying to decide which guys are going to make it next year and which aren't. What rookies will make the jump from the minors. What veterans will be sent out or released. We're sort of combination general managers and fortune tellers. We have to guess what an organization has on its mind. Will a manager want to carry three catchers this year? Can a guy fill in at several infield positions? We make out sample rosters using statistics from the league offices. Believe me, it's an extremely involved procedure. Sometimes I feel like a big league scout myself. And to tell you the truth, I think we usually do a better job than the organizations themselves—in predicting a particular club's 40-man roster. I think that's because we can afford to be a little more objective."

The shelves in his office are full of statistical manuals: "The Baseball Register," "The Baseball Encyclopedia," "The Sporting News Yearbooks." He keeps a running tab on each player's career—sort of a one-man band of the professional scouting combines.

"After we have decided who we are going to do cards on, we have to settle on a particular format for the year. We have eight people in the Sports Department altogether, and each of us is in on the decision. We have two contract photographers, three field reps, a sports card editor, a person who handles nothing but contracts, and myself. We like to change the cards around as much as possible from year to year, because, you see, we are basically in the children's entertainment business. When we have settled on a format for the cards, then we get to work immediately on the production. Most of the pictures have been taken the previous year—at spring training or some time during the season. We go through our files and pick out the best pictures. We have dozens of pictures of each major league ballplayer and we're very fussy about the ones that we use. We'll sometimes send our photographer back several times if we're not satisfied with what he might have gotten. It's a lot different from the way that it used to be when we had only one photographer on a part-time basis. All the players used to come out in the same poses—catchers with their fists clenched, managers yelling out instructions. The same things over and over again. It was embar-

24

rassing. Now we can be proud of our pictures. We've got some of the best sports photography in the business."

There are pictures all over the office—on the walls, on the desks, in folders and boxes. There are a dozen pictures of Willie Mays in his new Mets uniform, smiling, swinging a fungo bat, making basket catches.

"Then we begin writing the copy. We used to have some very big sportswriters working for us. I could tell you names that would really surprise you. But now we're back to doing it all ourselves—although with a considerably enlarged staff from before. I like to put out a lot of body copy—interesting anecdotes, little sidelights about the different players. But the kids are in love with statistics. So of course we have to give them what they want. We check every statistic over and over again and we seldom, if ever, make a mistake.

"After that, the cards are sent over to the Art Department where they are cut and pasted up and finished off. We have a whole staff of commercial artists and graphic designers working on every aspect of our various novelty products. They draw Bazooka comics, design wrappers, illustrate cartoons. Several of them work full time on our sports cards. Here's a series we did last year—childhood pictures of major league ballplayers."

He hands a stack of cards over the desk to me. The "Boyhood Photos of the Stars." Jim Fregosi smiling and playing the accordian. Willie Stargell in his Little League uniform.

"These went over very well. I was quite surprised. We're planning to do even more of them this year. After that it's all in the hands of our manufacturing department, although I keep a close watch on all the procedures. But I have to begin supervising the production of our other sports cards, too—football, basketball, and hockey. We're not just in the baseball card business you know, although baseball cards account for 60 percent of our sports volume. We sold 20 million packages of baseball cards last year and almost 200 tons of bubble gum. They're 2½ to 1 over football cards, with basketball and hockey cards just about even. We've also started doing British football players in England and I suppose pretty soon we'll be doing Ping-Pong players from China. Around the first of the year the cards are ready for manufacture and they hit the street the first week in March. The bubble gum season extends from March to early September, when the kids are out playing on the streets. That's when we do the major part of our business, although we do have little peaks at Halloween and Christmas. And the kids are pretty tough customers, too, you know. They're pretty particular about how they spend their money. You wouldn't believe some of the letters we get on our cards. They pick out every little mistake and petty detail. It's not at all like dealing with a grownup market."

In 1939 Mickey tried out for the Giants as a pitcher.

He was advised to try the outfield and finally found his spot as a catcher. He started in organized ball with Trenton in 1941 and homered his first time at bat. The next three years he was in the Army and was captured by the Germans in North Africa.
—From the baseball card of Mickey Grasso, catcher, Washington Senators.

A tour of the Topps editorial offices is a jolt—a forced reentry into some idle childhood fantasy. The furnishings may seem to be low-rent-district industrial modern, but the attendant trappings are straight out of "Little Lulu." The air is sweet with the smell of fresh bubble gum. The reception room is full of giant boxes of candy. Kids' posters line the walls and the hallways. All the secretaries have bubble gum samples on their desks. Candy Apple. Gold Rush. Nickel Bozo. Green bubble gum. Red bubble gum. Blue. Sy Berger is our genial master of ceremonies. Willy Wonka in pale blue doubleknit.

"This is our Product Development Department, where we work on all of next season's products. We've had a 100 percent growth rate in the last six years. And this place has been primarily responsible."

A little room off to the side of the corridor, filled with oversized cartons of juvenilia. All the Topps products and apparently everybody else's. Cut and twisted into every possible configuration. Good and Plenty. Jujy Fruits. Nestlé's Crunch Bars. The whole room agog with sweet and playful junk; on the desks, on the floors, on the windowsills. Ludwig Von Drake gone just slightly off his top.

"And this is our Art Department here. Sort of the nerve center of the whole operation. We have a dozen people working here full time. On every aspect of our graphic production."

Men bent over canted easels in tortured positions—like little elves finishing up on Christmas Eve—pasting strips of statistics to an oversized dummy baseball card, airbrushing blemishes off of Diego Segui.

"I'm very proud of what we've been able to do here. We've even put Bazooka comics out in foreign languages."

He reaches out for a strip of wax paper wrappers. And sure enough there is Pesky gagging it up in German:

> Warum der je wohl Hippopotamus heist?
> Sie weiler so wie eins aussieht.
> Heh. Heh. Heh. Heh. Heh. Heh. Heh. Heh.

An offer for a Flemish Bazooka Club emblem:

> Word ook lid van de Bazooka-Club, Stur je nam, adres en gaborte-datum. Doe er 5 bazookawikkels en 1 postzegel van 12 CT BJJ, dan clubsigne van Bazooka Joe, Postbus 1107, Den Haag.

Even a bilingual "Learn French with Bazooka Joe":

—Tu sais, Joe, il y a beaucoup de filles qui n'aiment pas sortir avec
garçons! (You know, Joe, lots of girls don't like to go out on dates.)
—Comment sais-tu, Mort? (How do you know, Mort?)
—Je leur ai demandé. (Because I asked them.)

"That's the sort of thing we've been able to accomplish here. Something you wouldn't have dreamed of only a few short years ago. And it's the sort of thing that makes me proud to be with Topps, to be associated with such a forward-looking organization."

His voice assumes an almost somber baronial resonance. His eyes seem to glaze over with the wonder of it all. Yet there is an unmistakable sincerity in his tone. A genuine commitment to the notion of perpetual childhood.

"You know I think it's important to be good at what you do. And there's no question in my mind that Topps is the best."

Out now into the sales and executive area. But even here the grade school trappings do not subside. Reproductions of old baseball cards in every direction—as well as samples of all the other collector cards.

"We've done cards on just about every conceivable subject—Davy Crockett, Hopalong Cassidy, Elvis Presley, antique railroads, fighter planes, the Beatles. We've had cards on all the really major television shows. 'Gunsmoke.' 'Batman.' 'The Partridge Family.' We've been years ahead of our time on every one of them. You have to anticipate way ahead on these things. You have to work out a particular trend before it breaks."

There is a new series right now on the drawing board—cards involving puns on well-known brand-name products. "Slumber Bread." "Threaded Wheat." "Coo-Coo Cola." The creative wheels at Topps grind exceedingly small.

"I think the main thing that makes our cards so successful is their completeness. And our very close attention to physical detail. Last year we printed 787 different baseball cards and you wouldn't believe the amount of labor that went into them. A kid picks up a package of cards in some variety store, he has no idea of the kind of detail work involved. But of course it all pays off for us in the long run. It's not something other card companies have been noted for."

Sy Berger could name some names if he wanted to. But he prefers to keep his counsel on this subject.

"Collecting cards goes back almost a hundred years. We have a guy working here who has a great collection. They used to have cards of Civil War heroes and Indian chiefs. They started giving them away at first with cigar packages. The first baseball cards were put out by Old Judge cigarettes. That was in 1886. The most famous was the Sweet Caporal line. They did all their printing on sepia paper with studio poses of all the different players. The players came through bug-eyed from the popping of the flash powder. The guys from Sweet Caporal are the ones who put out the Honus

Wagner card in 1910 without even getting Wagner's permission. He didn't smoke and he objected to their using his picture to sell cigarettes so they had to withdraw it almost immediately. There are only seven in existence today and they're each supposed to be worth about $1,500. The Metropolitan Museum of Art has the biggest collection of baseball cards in the world — almost 100,000. They got it from some guy in Syracuse."

He shakes his head while imparting this information. Whether at the number, or at Syracuse, it is hard to tell.

"There have been a lot of companies in it through the years. Diamond Stars. Goudey Gum. Fleer and Bowman. I used to collect the Goudey cards myself. They used to put out both major and minor leaguers. I had 249 out of their 250 cards. The only guy I couldn't get was Jess Petty. I finally found another kid who had him, but he wouldn't make a deal of any kind. I don't think I've really ever gotten over it completely."

And it is clear from the way he says this that it is true.

"There have been all sorts of other baseball cards, too. Cards on the backs of cereal boxes, cards on soft drink caps, and milk cartons. There have even been baseball cards built inside of marbles. But we're really the only ones serious about it these days.

He pauses momentarily in respectful memory of dear departed Goudey and Bowman.

"I get calls all the time from different people, asking how they can get complete collections of cards. I have to tell them I have absolutely no idea. When Bowie Kuhn asked me for a set of Topps cards a few years ago I had to buy one from an ad in 'The Sporting News.' We don't do any selling directly to collectors. We're only interested in doing business with kids."

And now down the hallway again, past storage rooms full of Bazooka, to the picture room where all the sports files are kept. Metal cabinets full of photographs old and current. Frank Robinson's file several inches thick.

"Frank Bertaina? What's he doing in here. Pete Cimino? Frank Thomas? Bobby Tiefenauer? One of these days we're going to have to get current. Look, here's a picture of Bruce Swango of the Orioles. He's the bonus baby they gave a hundred grand to, then discovered he couldn't pitch in front of crowds. Too nervous. We never even used him. We never use a lot of these pictures. Pat Bourque? There's a kid I really can't figure. Got all the tools but he can't get out of the minors. Chicago organization. Signed in 1969. Here's Enos Cabel, a kid out of Puerto Rico with Baltimore. The kid looks like he's probably going to make it. We've got one of the biggest sports picture libraries in the country. We practically make up the first six months of 'Sports Illustrated.' Look, here's a sheet of next year's cards. Aren't they a beautiful sight to behold?"

He holds them fondly, almost tenderly, at arm's length. They seem to glisten as he cradles them in his palms. And they are beautiful, more beautiful than in memory.

28

Clear and vivid and more colorful than ever before.

"This is the best series I think we've ever done. I'm very excited about the whole thing already."

Down the hall now toward the executive offices. Quiet and somber and gleaming with richly polished wood. A bust of Franklin Roosevelt at the entrance to the president's office. In front of him a wax carton of Bazooka. And then finally into the employee cafeteria. Where the special today is spiced sausage meat and rice. Bazooka news all over the employees' cork bulletin board. Sy Berger eating a bowl of cottage cheese.

> A mail carrier during the off-season, Johnny hopes to carry a full share of the Cubs' victories this year. He got his first Big League Trial with the Cubs in 1950 and although he had a 2-9 record, this was improved in 1951. In 2 years, he's beaten the Braves 4 times.
> — From the 1953 baseball card of Johnny Klippstein, pitcher, Chicago Cubs.

"My friends are always coming up to me and saying, 'Sy, every kid in America envies your job.' I say — 'I've got news for you, Pal. I envy my job myself.'"

We are safely back in the Sports Department now, among the baseball things that are Sy Berger's first love. The huge cardboard blowups of Topps minor league trophies. The reproductions of the college and high school All Star teams. It is getting on into the late afternoon and the workday is slowly winding its way down. Sy Berger has skipped his customary after-lunch nap, although he seems very little the worse for wear. Sitting back in his little sporting cubbyhole now, amidst the ephemera of his twenty years of baseball cards, it seems easy to understand why he is envied, why he might seem to have the best job in the world. And why, lulled by the sheer mellowness and contentment of it all, he can pause briefly for a few reminiscences.

"I was born in a pretty rough neighborhood in the Bronx about ten blocks or so from Yankee Stadium. Every day we used to go to see a ballgame, either to the Polo Grounds or up the street to see the Yankees. But for some reason I've always been a Boston fan. In baseball and every other sport. Either because my family first lived there when they came over from the old country or because the Braves had an outfielder named Wally Berger. I've never really been sure which it was. But after all these years my favorite player is still Ted Williams. Absolutely the greatest natural hitter there ever was. Teddy was very instrumental in helping us get started, incidentally. Here, I've got a letter from him somewhere on my desk."

He flips quickly through a great mound of papers. There does not appear to be any chance that he will find it.

"I'll find it later on if you'd like to see it. Anyway, I graduated from P.S. 64 and then went on to DeWitt Clinton High School. A pretty ordinary New York childhood I would say, nothing outstanding or extraordinary about it. And then on to Bucknell University and then into the Army at the start of the war. When I got out, I got a job at B. Altman's as a salesman, while I went to N.Y.U. nights. I came to Topps in 1947 to run a promotion for a couple of months. And I've been here, of course, ever since. I was made sales manager a few years after I came, and when the baseball thing opened up I jumped right in. I really didn't have that much working knowledge of sports, although I was sports editor of my division newspaper in the Air Force. I also played a little ball myself as a kid but nothing good enough to get me anywhere."

Like all of us when we are forced to say this sort of thing, he cannot quite camouflage all of his regret.

"The only ballplayer I ever knew personally was Bob Keegan, who I went to school with in Pennsylvania. But naturally we all learn about these things as we go along and, on the whole, I'd say that things couldn't have worked out better. Until not too long ago I was still the sales manager and running the Sports Department at the same time. But it was just getting to be absolutely too much and so I gave up the sales end of things."

He pauses momentarily and gazes up at the ceiling, like a man reflecting briefly on his past.

"I had to ask myself, 'Do I really want to be the sports picture card director of a bubble gum company?' And I guess the answer just turned out to be yes. I mean I have a great time doing what I do and that's the most important thing in my book. I may not be the richest guy in the world and maybe I could have done better financially in some other area. But this is the thing that I love. And there aren't too many guys who can say that."

The smile reappears beneath the smooth suntan. Lingering doubts and backward glances quickly dispelled.

"So what else can I tell you. I live in Rockville Centre, Long Island, with my wife and my children and my two dogs. I come into work every day in a car pool, five days a week, nine until five, just like a million other guys. I go to a lot of banquets and testimonials representing the company. That's a big part of my job, representing baseball and Topps to the public. And I travel about thirteen weeks out of every year, just to make sure all my ballplayers are happy. I always make it down to spring training and manage to see each player while I'm down there. I visit the locker room of each visiting team at least once every time they're in New York. I go to the World Series, the All Star game, the draft meetings. Any place there are baseball people, that's where I'll be. And I've finally become a New York fan. Although I'd appreciate it if you wouldn't let it get around."

Sy Berger is devoted indeed to his sports cards. And he is enthusiastic to a fault about bubble gum. But it is baseball that really demands his loyalty. All his conversations are channeled toward the subject.

"When I first came here I was very interested in baseball. But now it's just about become my whole life. I think it's the greatest game in the world—bar none. And I can't think of anything more satisfying than following it."

There doesn't seem to be anything that he doesn't know about the game. No player is too obscure for his memory. He is a walking encyclopedia of baseball knowledge. Vital statistics seem to flow from him like wine.

"The best thing is getting to know the guys. Visiting with them. Kidding them. Listening to their problems. I am personally friendly with almost every guy in the game. To me they're friends, they're not just celebrities. Willie Mays is probably the best friend I've got. I've got the keys to his apartment in my pocket. An amazingly sensitive man for such a famous athlete—a guy with a rare and quiet gift for human friendship. And Billy Pierce who's the kind of guy everybody likes and, of course, Williams and Kiner and Kluszewski. Current players. Retired players. All of them. I see them every day, talk to them on the telephone, even lend them money. To me they're just like my sons. Even Jim Bouton and Jim Piersall, guys I've had differences with—even these guys I respect for what they are. Even the guys who are always bugging me about their pictures. Listen, you wouldn't believe how vain some of these guys are. Willie Mays is almost never happy with his pictures. I always have to send the photographer back for more. I say to him—'Willie, did you ever take a good look at yourself in the mirror? You can't make a silk purse out of a sow's ear, you know.' The only guy I know who really liked his pictures was Don Maynard of the Jets. He called me up once and ordered a duplicate set for his mother. But I don't mind. Even the guys who used to sign contracts with our competition and then come around and sign another contract with us. Joe Garagiola looked me right in the eye and told me he had not signed another contract with anyone else, and all the time I had a duplicate of his Bowman contract right on my desk. What a guy."

He smiles and laughs and points over to the corner. There is a bronze trophy there in the shape of a top hat. It is about the size of a small water heater. It says: "With Grateful Appreciation to Joe Garagiola. The First and Only All Time All Star Rookie." Sy Berger knows when he is being kidded. But a baseball player can get away with an awful lot with him.

"I wouldn't trade places with anyone in the world. This is the kind of job you couldn't even invent."

And sitting there it is not all that hard to believe. In the middle of this bubble gum factory in Brooklyn. With Big Buddy and Gold Rush coming at you from everywhere. With Bazooka Joe and his gang an unspeaking presence. With baseball cards surrounding you and enfolding you. And autographed 8 x 10's of all the current stars. Pasted and taped into cardboard folders on filing cabinets. Because Sy Berger hasn't had time to put them up yet. And Sy Berger, himself, with his all-consuming love of baseball. The children's game that some lucky children never outgrow.

31

"The thing about baseball is that it's really a classic game. It changes somewhat, but it never seems to change. And a kid can readily identify with a ballplayer. They're not terribly tall or physically enormous. A kid can look at one of our cards and see himself. See himself standing like that, or fielding like that. It's not a game for freaks or guys with unusual talents. It's a game that almost anyone can play. And every year you never know what's going to happen. You never know what new stars will come along. Will Carleton Fisk be as good as Bill Dickey? Will Hank Aaron break Babe Ruth's home run record? Our cards used to be five for a nickel. Now they come in packages of ten for a dime. Some things change but the basics remain the same. Our cards are always going to be around. And that's the way it is with baseball too. Every season some unexpected things will happen. Look at Steve Carlton and Cesar Cedeno last year. That's what makes it worth our while. None of us knows who's really going to make it. Although a lot of guys like to pretend that they know. What new rookie will come out of the minor leagues? What good pitcher will lose some speed off his fast ball? We've had our eyes on all these players ever since we signed them. But we don't know and nobody else knows either. That's what makes the whole thing so fascinating. You know basically what to expect, but not the specifics. Here's Mario Guerrero, a kid from the Dominican Republic. Signed with the Yankees a few years ago. A great fielder but not much with the bat. The Yankees threw him to Boston in the Sparky Lyle deal. The Red Sox didn't even know who he was. Strictly extra baggage. Now all of a sudden he's hitting .320 in winter ball. He looks like he's ready, but how can you tell? He had a good year at Louisville but that doesn't mean much. There're so many things to be taken into consideraion. Will Luis Aparicio last another year? Can they steady down their other kid, Beniquez? Would they want to leave Guerrero on the bench? He's got a lot of ability and he could make the jump. He's very young and he's improving all the time. Of course he could have a terrible spring training, too. That's another thing you have to consider. I got a feeling that this kid is going to make it though. I could be wrong. Because you never really know. It's always a tough step up that last rung of the ladder. It's going to be very interesting to see what he can do."

Here's a collection of earlier cards.

"TOM" SUNKEL

"ARKY" VAUGHAN

No, they don't make them like this anymore.

Profiles

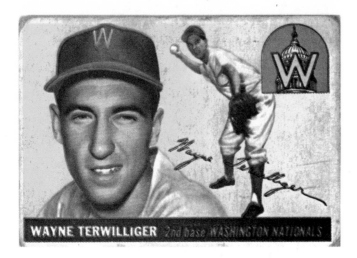

Everybody remembers Wayne Terwilliger. But nobody can remember exactly why. Wayne was the perfect utility man. He couldn't hit his hat size, but he could field every position. He wouldn't help you out very much, but he wouldn't embarrass you either. He had a good disposition, was always sober, and liked to pitch batting practice—in other words, a manager's dream. He also looked like a utility man—he had a utility man's face, a utility man's build, and a utility man's outlook on life. And certainly no one could argue the fact that he had a utility man's name. He always looked to me like the sort of guy you might send for to unplug a drain in a large apartment house. Of course, what made it even better was that he played with some of the worst Washington Senator teams of the early fifties, teams consisting of entire rosters of utility men.

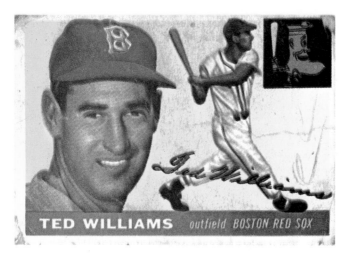

In 1955 there were 77,263,127 male American human beings.

And every one of them in his heart of hearts would have given two arms, a leg, and his collection of Davy Crockett iron-ons to be Teddy Ballgame.

Choo Choo Coleman was the quintessence of the early New York Mets. He was a 5′8″, 160-pound catcher who never hit over .250 in the majors, had 9 career home runs, 30 career RBIs, and couldn't handle pitchers. Plus his name was Choo Choo. What more could you ask for?

Vern Stephens hit pop-ups.

   High pop-ups. Major league pop-ups. Neck straining pop-ups.

   Pop-ups which often disappeared from sight. Pop-ups which on occasion brought rain.

   For this reason he was known as Pop-Up Stephens —logically and concisely enough.

   Except to those who already knew him as Junior.

   Vern Stephens, it has often been said, could have played his entire career in a stovepipe.

   If they could have found a stovepipe wide enough to hold him.

Some more funny-things-you-can-do-with-Louisville-sluggers department.

On August 22, 1965, Juan Marichal, the Giants' star pitcher, efficiently and unexpectedly cold-cocked John Roseboro, the Dodger's star catcher, with his 36-ounce white ash Adirondack. For this "unprovoked and obnoxious" assault Marichal was fined $1,750, suspended for nine days, and made to write fifty times on the blackboard in Warren Giles' office, "I will never again attempt to rearrange a fellow player's hair style without first obtaining that player's permission." Roseboro, for his part, from that time forward wore the peculiarly eye-popping, air-sucking, and perpetually astonished expression he displays for you here in this photograph.

Whoooooooooooeeeeeeeeeeeeeeeeee.

Charlie Smith was a very ordinary third baseman for the Cardinals in the mid-sixties. The only extraordinary thing about Charlie was that when the Yankees went to trade Roger Maris in 1966, only two years after he had broken Babe Ruth's home run record, Charlie Smith was all they could get for him. That should tell you something although I'm not sure exactly what.

Even if you didn't follow baseball you knew about Bo Belinsky. But I bet you didn't know that his first name was Robert.

Bo spent six years in the minors before coming up to the Angels in 1962, toiling anonymously in leaky-roofed bucolic outposts such as Pensacola and Brunswick, Aberdeen, and Amarillo, quaint little mid-American hamlets which, while not totally without their charms, I am sure, were nevertheless not exactly tailor-made for the kind of varied and far-reaching social activities that Bo liked to engage in.

When he got a shot at L.A., baby, he was ready.

He was the first of the rookie holdouts (Mike Epstein was the second) and the originator of the poolside spring training press conference for nonroster pitchers. He pitched a no-hitter one of his first times out, was rewarded with a new contract by Angels' owner Gene Autrey ("Rudolph, the Red-Nosed Reindeer," "If It Doesn't Snow on Christmas"), and was even engaged for a short time to Mamie Van Doren — no small accomplishment in itself.

It took about a year and a half for Bo and fellow fun-seeker, Dean Chance, to pool hustle, chug-a-lug, and peppermint twist their way into semiobsolescence, although Chance, whose heart never seemed quite as much in these quixotic recreational endeavors as did Bo's, did manage to salvage a few more good years with the Angels and the Twins. Bo was still active, in more ways than one I'm sure, as late as 1969 with Hawaii of the Pacific Coast League. What he could have done in baseball had he been serious about the whole thing is an entertaining speculation, but since Bo didn't really seem to have cared, why should we?

PITCHER
BO BELINSKY

The 1969 baseball card of Aurelio Rodriguez is not Aurelio Rodriguez at all but the Pittsburgh Pirate bat boy. This is in the nature of a little joke by Aurelio who could very easily be mistaken for a bat boy, except that most bat boys could easily outhit him.

And were considerably more mature in the bargain.

If you feel that Dave DeBusschere is a great athlete then you are definitely better off never having seen him play baseball.

Oooopppps!

In 1963 while pitching for Milwaukee, the fourth of his seven major league teams, Bob Shaw committed 8 balks – 5 in one game, 3 in one inning.

Pretty silly.

Sam Jethroe, Jet for short, had a brief four-year career with Boston and Pittsburgh, and if he did nothing spectacular, he was nevertheless one of the few black players in the league, a pacesetter who's pretty much forgotten now, but whose courage as a pioneer under difficult circumstances it is good and necessary to recall and pay tribute to.

Boyd Gail Harris – whose name has obvious meaning for the authors – took over a first base from Whitey Lockman in 1955 for the Giants. He finished a short career with the Detroit Tigers in 1960. Fred Harris I could understand. But Boyd Gail Harris?

Van Lingle Mungo is the only player in the history of major league baseball to have a popular song written about him. With the possible exception of Blue Moon Odom and Sonny Siebert.

Woodie Held is the all-time strike-out per at bats leader of the major leagues with an average of .235. He is followed closely by Frank Howard with an average of .233. After this comes Harmon Killebrew, Mickey Mantle, Bob Allison, Wally Post, Lou Brock, Larry Doby, Willey McCovey, Gus Zernial, Dolf Camili, Jim Landis, Leo Cardenas, Eddie Mathews, Duke Snider, Norm Siebern, Dick McAuliffe, Tom Tresh, Clete Boyer, Hank Greenberg, Johnny Callison, Gil Hodges, Jimmie Foxx, Joe Adcock, and Jim Fregosi.

The fact that all but three of these players were active during the fifties and sixties will tell you something, I think, about the times in which we live.

Hey, Howard, you can still catch up if you hurry.

INF-OUTFIELD
WOODY HELD

Gail Harris

1st BASE   DETROIT TIGERS

"VAN" MUNGO

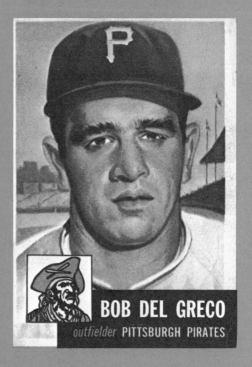

You see my problem was that I always thought that Mike de la Hoz **was** Bobby Del Greco. And vice versa. I had much the same problem with Gerry Staley and Jerry Priddy, Joe Pignatano and Joey Amalfitano, Howie Pollett and Erv Palica and Billy Hunter and Billy Gardner. To say nothing of Walter Dukes and Ray Felix—but of course that's a whole separate problem entirely. So anyway, what I want to know now is, if Mike de la Hoz is not Bobby Del Greco, then who, if anybody, is he?

Minnie Minoso played the game the way it's supposed to be played. He did not have the power of a Mantle or the overall talent of a Mays, but he sprayed hits to all fields, never swung at a bad pitch, crowded the plate, bunted, stole bases, broke up double plays, made diving catches, and always, but always, hit the cut-off man. He loved to play baseball, was in every minute of every game he ever played and never let up, no matter how one-sided the score. He was what baseball was all about and, as a matter of fact, he still is what baseball is all about. Because last year at an age when most baseball players have resigned themselves to placid careers of fly-tying and package store operation, Minnie Minoso was one of the leading hitters in the Mexican League. And by Jesus I bet he can still do everything as well as he ever did.

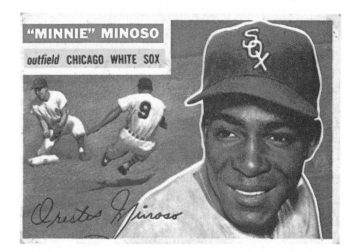

"MINNIE" MINOSO
outfield CHICAGO WHITE SOX

YANKEES

PHIL LINZ   inf-of

Phil Linz gained a certain notoriety during the early sixties for four distinct, if dubious, accomplishments, none of which had anything to do with his baseball career.

First was his partnership in the New York dating bar, Bachelors Three.

Second was his close friendship with, and emulation of, the noted Alabama social critic and cultural historian, Joe Namath.

Third was the impression engendered in the hearts of all true Yankee-haters everywhere, by his mere presence in the New York lineup, that the end of the Yankee Golden Era had finally arrived.

And fourth, but certainly not least, was his harmonica-playing wizardry, which, when engaged in on the back of the Yankee team bus after a particularly galling New York defeat, so infuriated General Manager Ralph Houk that he was moved not only to fine Linz quite heavily but also to threaten to tear him limb from limb were he ever faced with a recurrence of such spontaneous musical virtuosity.

Phil, of course, cooled it immediately and went on to hit a staunch .207 that year before being traded to the Phillies for a bag of broken bats and a pop-up toaster. Philly manager Gene Mauch was rumored to have a soft spot in his heart for musically inclined second basemen. Phil pined for the bright lights of Broadway though, and his career, such as it was, languished. By 1968 he had played himself out of baseball entirely.

Roger Craig was a pretty fair pitcher for the Dodgers for seven years before being drafted by the Mets in 1962. In that year his record was 10–24. He followed this in 1963 with a 5–22 season before being mercifully traded to the Cardinals. Like Dizzy Dean used to say, though, it takes a pretty good pitcher to lose 20 games a year in the majors, and Roger was rewarded for his long suffering by being named the Mets' pitching coach in 1967. This perhaps accounts for the bemused expression on his face in this card.

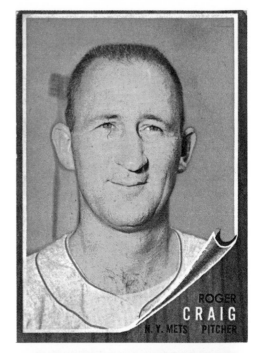

Ryne Duren was a relief pitcher for the Yankees for three years in the late fifties. He was what the sportscasters like to refer to as a fireballing right-hander, a real flamethrower, an aspareeen chucker. In other words he could really bring it. He also annually led the league in bad eyesight. He wore milk-bottle-thick, tinted glasses and he used to warm up before each inning by throwing a series of particularly nasty overhand fast balls into the ground in front of home plate, over the catcher's head, against the backstop, and into the stands. Not exactly the type of behavior likely to instill confidence in the hearts of prospective batters. Unfortunately, like most hard-throwing relief pitchers—Joe Black, Joe Page, Dick Radatz, et al.—his arm began to give out shortly after he learned to control his fast ball, and he spent his last few years in baseball trying to hang on with a succession of mediocre teams in both leagues.

As in many other areas of organizational ineptitude, in promoting catching mediocrity the New York Mets cared enough to send the very worst. It was apparently George Weiss' feeling that if something was worth doing, it was worth doing poorly, and if he was going to collect a stinko corps of catchers, then by God it was really going to be a stinko corps of catchers. Therefore the receiving staffs of the first several editions of the Mets included in their number the likes of Joe Ginsberg, Joe Pignatano, Sammy Taylor, Hobie Landrith, Norm Sherry, Clarence (Choo Choo) Coleman, Harry Chiti, and Chris Cannizzaro. Not exactly a collection of names likely to threaten the memory of Gabby Hartnett, or even Buddy Rosar for that matter. I always wondered how they managed to miss out on Danny Kravitz.

Landrith was the Mets' first draft choice in 1962 — which will give you some idea of the caliber of the talent available. Choo Choo Coleman was the young man who, when asked by Ralph Kiner in a postgame interview, "Choo Choo, how come people call you Choo Choo?" replied, "I don't know, Ralph." And Chris Cannizzaro was simply and definitively — Chris Cannizzaro. I'd like to be able to tell you who was the best of this motley crew, but in fact no one was. Way down underneath they were all really the same person.

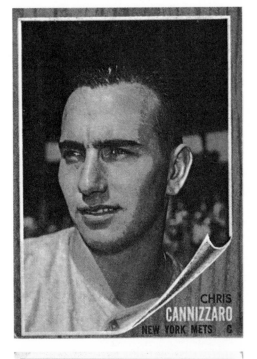

CHRIS CANNIZZARO
NEW YORK METS C

Four things and four things only do we know about Samuel Jones.

(1) That he was born in Stewartsville, Ohio, and lived in Monongah, West Virginia.

(2) That he never owned a hat that really fit him.

(3) That he had a toothpick surgically attached to his lower lip.

(4) And that if anyone ever deserved to be called Sad Sam, it was Sad Sam Jones of Monongah.

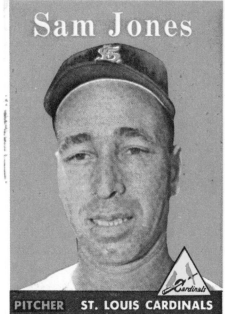

Sam Jones
PITCHER   ST. LOUIS CARDINALS

Bill Tuttle looked like the perfect answer to "What's the use." He was a starting outfielder for several seasons with the Detroit Tigers—a team painfully short of qualified starting outfielders—who was forced in 1961 to undergo the ultimate in baseball indignities—being sold by the ninth-place Kansas City Athletics to the seventh-place Minnesota Twins, who promptly tried to turn him into a third baseman. This is a little like being expelled from the Bowery for slovenliness and then deported to Denmark for a sex change operation. Bill was not actually as bad a ballplayer as he looked (this being a physical impossibility). But it was close. He led the American League in putouts in 1955 and 1960 which, Frank Lary and Billy Hoeft to the contrary, was more of a reflection on the Detroit and Kansas City pitching staffs than it was on Bill.

Cheer up there Bill. It's all over now.

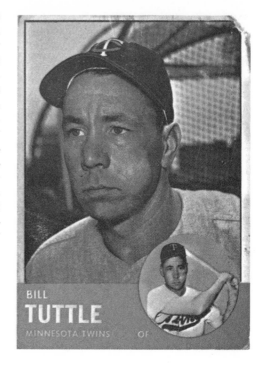

BILL
TUTTLE
MINNESOTA TWINS   OF

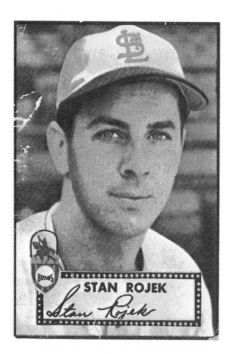

STAN ROJEK

If you search long enough and far enough you will discover that every major league ballplayer, no matter how inept or mediocre, holds some sort of absurdly obscure record. Gordon Goldsberry holds the record for the most errors in the third inning of the second game of a twilight doubleheader by a left-handed first baseman with an alliterative name. Rudy Minarcin holds the record for the long distance, wind-aided rosin bag throw by a Pennsylvania-born relief pitcher with a losing record. And Bobby Malkmus holds the record for the most vacant expression by an underweight utility infielder of Polish extraction with an I.Q. over 110.

Stan Rojek does hold a legitimate major league record as it happens, having taken part in five double plays in one game.

It's not much. But it beats having to work for a living.

We all make mistakes. Branch Rickey once touted Marvin Rackley as the "new Paul Waner." Rogers Hornsby thought Jim Rivera would burn up the major leagues. Joe McCarthy thought that Jack Phillips had the potential to be better than Marty Marion. The Yankee management called Jim Brideweser the greatest shortstop since Honus Wagner. And Leo Durocher predicted year after year that Gail Henley would become the best hitter in the majors. The young major league baseball prospect has a way of losing the bloom off his rose faster almost than you would think humanly possible. Like all those ingenues in the late forties' musicals who sink faster than a bowl of stale Wheat Chex.

Featuring Harvey Keck and Mary Louise Lovely. Introducing Terry Tide and Jennifer Jennerette.

The fifties had its share of unqualified duds. Tom Umphlett was supposed to make us forget about DiMaggio, Roger Repoz had it all over Tris Speaker. And Clint Hartung—the Hondo Hurricane—was a prospect of such fabled potential that Tom Meany thought he shouldn't even bother to stop at the Polo Grounds but should report straight to Cooperstown instead. They didn't call Clint "Floppy" for nothing.

Frank Leja was a massive young power-hitting first baseman whom the Yankees signed for a huge bonus in 1953. According to the publicity releases he could hit like Johnny Mize and field like Dick Sisler. As it turned out he hit like Casey Wise and fielded like Dick Stuart.

Dear Ma, I'll probably be home some time next week. They're starting to throw me the curve ball.

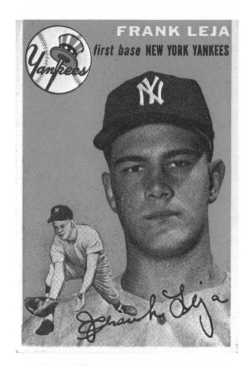

Willie Jones was nicknamed "Puddin' Head" after a song popular during his youth, and the name was somehow appropriate as a description of this slow-moving third baseman from South Carolina. His outstanding play around third base for the 1950 Phillies, particularly in a losing effort in the World Series, made up for his sluggish batting.

Some players play in the wrong era.
Some players play with the wrong team.
Some players play the wrong position.

Charlie Silvera somehow managed all three. Charlie Silvera played nine years for the Yankees in the fifties, during which time they won seven American League pennants. This enabled him to cash quite a few World Series checks, but it sure didn't help to get him into the lineup. Charlie twice led the Pacific Coast League in catching defense, had a .283 lifetime batting average, and hit .315 the only year he was up more than 100 times. But he had about as much chance of ousting Yogi Berra and Elston Howard for the starting Yankee roster as I do of replacing Prince Ranier. In ten years in the majors he was up 482 times. It isn't enough just to be good at what you do.

You also got to know how to pick your spots.

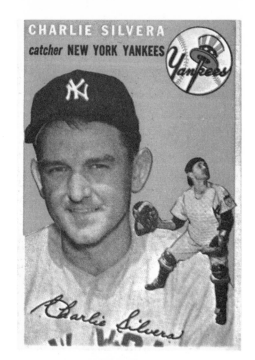

(1) Avoid fried meats which angry up the blood.
(2) If your stomach disputes you, lie down and pacify it with cool thoughts.
(3) Keep the juices flowing by jangling around gently as you move.
(4) Go very light on the vices such as carrying on in society; the social ramble ain't restful.
(5) Avoid running at all times.
(6) Don't look back; something might be gaining on you.

Satchel Paige could have been the greatest pitcher in major league history, if he'd been given the chance.

Don't look back, America, something might be gaining on you.

There are two kinds of ballplayers who manage to stay in the major leagues for any length of time without ever winning a permanent starting position. One is the good field, no hit type of player such as Willie Miranda, George Strickland, and Jim Finigan. The other is the good hit, no field type of player such as Bob Cerv, Jose Tartabull, and Carlos Paula. Carlos Paula's ability to hit the baseball (.314 lifetime minor league batting average) could never quite make up for his inability to catch it. Washington fans would shudder whenever the ball was hit his way. I myself was once witness to his mishandling of three consecutive fly balls in one inning, two of which fell for extra base hits. Carlos had good speed, excellent range, and he usually got a pretty good jump on the ball, but he could never quite seem to get the hang of catching the damned thing, and in an outfielder this can be a disheartening weakness. It was for Carlos. He hasn't been heard from since 1956.

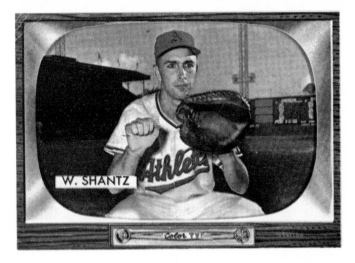

Around 1955 the creative people in the bubble gum game, starved as they were for new marketing and promotional techniques, decided that perhaps it was time to take advantage of the latest national craze — television. What was good enough for Milton Berle was certainly good enough for Bobo Newsom. Get a load of the fine wood grain paneling on this rig, the Sylvania Golden Glow picture tube, the sharply focused outline of the image, the words, "Color T.V." emblazoned in natural gold leaf on the luxurious control panel. This isn't just any ordinary old T.V. set you're fooling around with here, buster. This is the genuine article. The player in question is Wilmer Shantz, brother of Bobby Shantz, who although not as short as Bobby was not as good either. The last line on the back of the card says, "With Ottawa in 1953, Billy was in 105 games, batting .227." Things like that are best left unsaid.

There are certain ballplayers who are so colorless in their habits, so commonplace in their demeanor, so totally lacking in the essential dramatic fire of athletic combat that the best that anyone, even their most ardent admirers, can think to say about them is that they are steady. This means that they do not make too many errors, hit around .275, are always on time for the team bus and never forget their mother's birthday. Being considered steady is such a vaguely insulting characterization—somewhat akin to being thought of as "safe" by all the girls down at the bowling alley—that you might occasionally expect one of these sluglike individuals to resent it. They never seem to mind though. They're too steady.

The fifties were fraught with steady infielders—the infield being a particularly fertile breeding ground for steadiness—of all heights, weights, dispositions, and, curiously enough, abilities. Some of my favorites were: Andy Carey, who was married to a beauty queen; Bobby Doerr, who was from Los Angeles; Billy Goodman, whose middle name was Dale and who slouched; Ray Boone, who took over from Lou Boudreau and had bad knees; Woodie Held, who should have been an outfielder; Johnny Pesky, who batted in front of Ted Williams; Billy Martin, whose real name was Marchilengelo; Marty Marion, who was the world's tallest shortstop; Gene Mauch, who had a bad temper; Al Smith, who had beer poured on his head in the World Series; Jerry Lumpe, who had an unfortunate name; Norm Siebern, who was boring; Chuck Schilling, who was Carl Yastrzemski's roommate; George Kell, who batted over .300 nine times without anybody ever finding out; Johnny Lipon, whose nickname was "Skids"; and Jerry Adair who was nice.

But my favorite all-time imperturbable infielder was Eddie Bressoud, an itinerant shortstop of modest pretensions and equally modest accomplishments whose performances were so lacking in variation and whose character was so unflappable in crisis that he was finally gifted by his hordes of enthusiastic admirers with a nickname commensurate with his stress rate.

Yes, I'm afraid you're right—Steady Eddie.

EDDIE BRESSOUD   SS

coot veal

Orville Veal

DETROIT TIGERS
SHORTSTOP

Coot Veal?

Here's a real pip for you.

Jay Hook was a lanky engineering student from Waukeegan, Illinois, who looked like Wally Cleaver and pitched like Zasu Pitts. With the New York Mets teams of 1962–64 he compiled records of 8–19, 4–14, and 0–1, for a three-year cumulative total of 12–34, which might on the face of it seem rather horrendous unless you stopped to consider that Craig Anderson, the staff's beefy boy wunderkind in residence, had a record of 3–20 over the same time span and that Roger Craig, the stopper, if that is the proper phrase under the circumstances, had a two-year record of 15–46. The back of Jay's card is the very soul of discretion regarding these notable statistical deficiencies, stating in part: "Jay pitched better than his record indicated in '63." (All things taken into consideration he would have had a pretty tough time pitching any worse.) "Jay's a member of the National Rocket Society too!"

What could they possibly mean by "too"!

Hook once wrote an article for "Sport" magazine explaining why a curve ball curves. He had a hard time getting the message through to his arm though and was forced to retire in 1964 when he could no longer get even his own teammates out during spring training intersquad games. He spent eight years in the major leagues and never had a winning season. His final won-lost totals were 29–62, with a lifetime ERA of 5.23.

I'd sure as hell like to read a scientific explanation of that.

JAY
HOOK
NEW YORK METS PITCHER

John Berardino had an uneventful eleven-year career as a utility infielder with several American League teams. After he retired, however, he came into his own in show business as an actor in scores of grade-B Hollywood and TV gangster movies and westerns. He had one of the roughest faces this side of Sal Maglie, but as things developed, it looked better in a movie behind a gun than it did on the field behind third base. You've probably seen John many times, in old Superman episodes or on "The Untouchables" — he was the guy in the too big double-breasted suit, being knocked across the room by George Reeves or Robert Stack. Where is he now?

JOHN BERARDINO

Of course if you are really lousy at what you do, there's always a chance you can work your way into management. That being the American Way.

Walt Alston was up exactly once during his entire major league career. He struck out.

Sparky Anderson, on the other hand, managed to last a whole year with the Phillies in 1959, even though he batted only .218.

Then there was Paul Richards who in his eight-year National League career, most of which occurred during the war years, hit 15 home runs and had a lifetime batting average of .227.

Bucky Harris, Billy Southworth, Al Lopez, Jimmy Dykes, Chuck Dressen, Fred Haney, Steve O'Neil, Bobby Bragan, Bill Rigney and all the other paunchy, oracular guiding lights of the fifties did not exactly burn up the record books with their playing brilliance, either. Major league owners seem to prefer mediocrities in their managements. Feeling perhaps that the blind really do make the best leaders.

Harry Craft managed three teams in the majors over a seven-year span from 1957 to 1964. Not one of these teams had a winning record and their composite won-lost totals were 360–485. They finished 7th, 7th, 7th, 7th, 8th, 9th, and 9th. Do I detect a trend in there somewhere?

Les Moss has my all-time favorite major league managerial record. Acting as interim manager between Eddie Stankey and Al Lopez with the 1968 White Sox, Moss compiled a record of 0-2. 0-2. Perfection.

The Perfessor. I suppose that if there could be said to be an archetypal picture of Casey Stengel then this would have to be it. Don't give them too big a piece of your mind there, Casey, there's always the chance you might be needing it later on.

In six major league seasons Billy Muffett won 16 games while losing 23. He had a 4.33 lifetime ERA, gave up 407 hits, 132 walks, and had one shutout. In 1966 he was named pitching coach by the St. Louis Cardinals.

You figure it out.

Yes sir, Frankie Crosetti. Third base coach to the world. And if you really aren't too good at anything in particular there's always a chance for you to become an executive. That way you can spread your incompetence around a bit.

HARRY **CRAFT**
HOUSTON COLT .45s   MGR.

LES MOSS

MANAGER
CASEY STENGEL

FRANK CROSETTI

| BILLY MUFFETT | Boston |
| Pitcher | Red Sox |

WILLIAM HARRIDGE
PRESIDENT,
AMERICAN LEAGUE

WARREN GILES
PRESIDENT,
NATIONAL LEAGUE

Somewhere out there, between the magical mystical borderlines of Mudville and Cooperstown, there has to be a factory operating full time, turning out elongated and musclebound first basemen who bat left, throw left, hit for power, and can't field. This is one mold they don't seem to want to throw away.

Jim Gentile was 6′4″, weighed 215 pounds, and every year almost managed to make the number of runs he knocked in with his bat equal the number of runs he let in with his glove. He always looked to me like a low echelon commanding officer of a particularly inefficient Army unit who is about to leave the service after sixteen years in grade, with seven kids, a mortgaged trailer, and no pension, for a selling job with Standard Oil.

Earl Torgeson's two favorite activities were fist-fighting and breaking his shoulder, both of which he did whenever he got the chance. On the back of this card it says, "Torgy likes a good practical joke"— which is the biog writer's subtle way of suggesting that he enjoyed knocking people's teeth out. He is probably also the only left-handed hitting first baseman over 6′2″ who ever stole 20 bases in one season.

Some other members of the left-left club were Fred Whitfield, Bill White, George Crowe, Tim Harkness, Don Bollweg, and Marv Blaylock. We could include Ferris Fain and Mickey Vernon too, except that Ferris wasn't tall and Mickey had no muscles.

ATHLETICS

JIM GENTILE   1st base

Earl Torgeson

Everybody remembers Willie Mays' famous back-to-the-plate game-saving catch in the 1954 World Series. But nobody seems to remember that the catch was made off of Vic Wertz. Wertz was a good hit, no field, left-handed hitting first baseman with the Tigers and the Indians during the late forties and early fifties. In 1959 the Red Sox got him in a trade for Jim Piersall. Now in Boston, trading Jim Piersall is like the Vatican trading the Pietà. No matter what you get in return it isn't going to be enough. And Wertz did nothing to help the situation, either, by spending every other day for the next three seasons out of the lineup with a pulled muscle. This despite the fact that he did not seem to have any muscles to pull. In 1955 he finished third in the league in five o'clock shadow to Sal Maglie and Don Mossi.

According to the Peter Principle, the upward mobility of the individual corporate employee in the American free enterprise system is based on his mastering of succeeding levels of competence while progressing on to his ultimate level of incompetence—that area where the depth and range of his responsibilities are simply too great for the scope of his talents. For Steve Bilko the entire major league infrastructure was that level of incompetence. If Rochester was New York City, Steve Bilko would be in the Hall of Fame.

But it isn't.

And he isn't.

Big Steve tore apart the Piedmont League but he couldn't get arrested in the bigs. The first and last lines on the back of this card tell it all. "Hailed as another Jimmy Foxx in 1945. Had the second highest number of RBIs in the history of the Carolina League. In 1949 hit four homers in one day. Optioned to Rochester in 1952."

I wonder who had the highest number of RBIs in the history of the Carolina League.

56

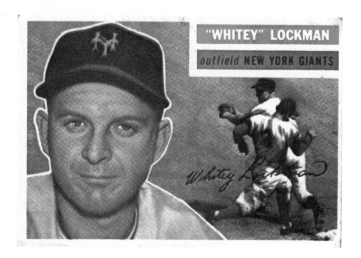

Whitey Lockman was the Giants' mainstay first baseman in the fifties, hardly ever missing a game, and always hitting around .300. He was the kind of player
managers love to have on their teams — steady, sober,
and a stabilizing influence on the other players. You
had the feeling that Whitey was somehow born responsible, the leader of his nursery school class, and
the kind of kid who never got into any kind of trouble.
He recently took over as manager of the Cubs when
Leo Durocher left, and you can be certain that his
players will perform well for him.

You could always count on Richie Ashburn. Lead-off
batter for the Whiz Kid Phillies of 1950, he was always getting on base. Over the course of a long
career he hit only 29 home runs, but his lifetime batting average was .308. He was the kind of player a
manager loves to have on his team: spirited, smart,
well conditioned, and a natural team leader. He deserved more than the one championship season
he got.

Despite all apparent evidence to the contrary, there
has never been, nor could there ever be, a major
league ballplayer named Clyde Kluttz.

Dusty Rhodes was one of those players whose medi-ocre career was almost redeemed by one, bright moment of glory. Dusty had been a reserve out-fielder, slow-moving and of no special grace. But for the New York Giants in the 1954 World Series against Cleveland, he won the first game with a tenth-inning home run with two on. His pinch-hit single tied the second game in the fifth, and his home run won it. In game three, Dusty pinch hit two runs home to in-sure victory, and in the fourth game he rested, as his teammates took over and swept the Indians. Dusty had one-third of his team's World Series RBIs, went 4-for-6, and had two home runs, and won a Corvette from "Sport" magazine, which I suspect he's still driving.

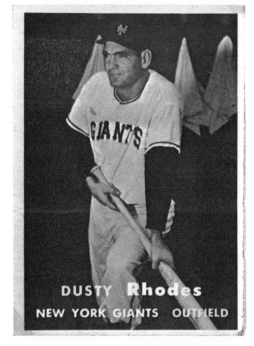

Herbie Plews is perhaps my favorite all-time second-rate ballplayer, just nosing out Chi Chi Olivo, and Lou "The Nervous Greek" Skizas. There was something almost heroic about the stupefying mediocrity of his play, the polished and studied indifference of his skills, which could, on occasion, move me almost to the brink of religious ebullition. It's no use trying to explain this feeling — you'd really have to have been there to appreciate it.

Suffice it to say that if Richard Nixon could play baseball he'd play like Herbie Plews.

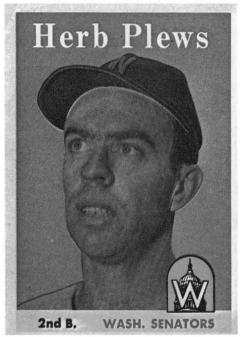

In four major league seasons, from 1957 to 1960, Casey Wise had batting averages of .179, .197, .171, and .147, or a four-year composite of .174. He was up 321 times, had 12 extra-base hits and 17 RBIs. In 1958 with Milwaukee he was up 71 times without knocking in a run. This may not be the worst major league hitting record of all time, but it's definitely in contention.

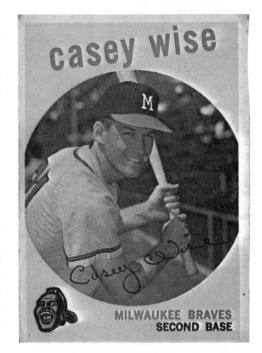

MILWAUKEE BRAVES
SECOND BASE

Twice and only twice in my many years of watching major league baseball have I been tempted to run out onto the playing field. The first time was during a game between the Angels and the Red Sox in July of 1959 when, incensed by the paralyzing ineptitude of the Boston bullpen, I was tempted to run out and perform a citizen's arrest on Murray Wall, the Red Sox relief pitcher, and charge him with impersonating a baseball player.

The second time was when I saw Stu Miller for the first time.

Stu Miller threw the ultimate banana ball. You had time for a Coke and a sandwich while waiting for his fast ball to arrive. His pitches took so long to get up to the plate in fact that they occasionally even appeared to be going backward. Watching him from behind the third base dugout was guaranteed to make your palms itch and your seat squirm. You wanted to hightail it on down to the bat rack and have a rip at the little guy yourself. It was all an optical illusion of course. You couldn't have hit him and neither could very many real ballplayers. His pitches may have looked like custard pies on the way up to the plate but they had a tendency to disappear when they arrived.

It all caught up with him in the 1961 All Star game, though: while pitching into the aberrated air currents of San Francisco's Candlestick Park, he became the first pitcher in modern baseball history to be blown off the mound by a gust of wind. Stick that in your old ephus ball Stu. You little bundle of meaningless motions.

STU MILLER
Pitcher   San Francisco Giants

One of the favorite games of my youth, which, incidentally, is still very much in progress, was called "lousy catcher," or "Charlie Lau." The object of this game was to name a major league catcher who was still more or less active and whose overall playing ability left, to say the least, quite a good deal to be desired. Once you had submitted the name of your choice—say, for example, Hank Foiles—your opponent had exactly five seconds to name a player of equal, or, if possible, inferior accomplishment—say, for example, Charlie Lau. The first participant who could not come up with a suitable candidate in the allotted time span was declared the loser. The winner's prize was an all-expenses-paid evening of dining and dancing with Matt Batts' sister.

Here is a list of my favorite submissions as well as the responses they generally elicited.

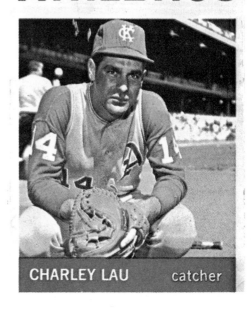

ATHLETICS

CHARLEY LAU   catcher

Joe Tipton—Owen Friend
Dixie Howell—Rube Walker
Len Okrie—Les Moss
Del Wilbur—Mickey Grasso
Joe Astroth—Valmy Thomas
Cal Neeman—Hal Naragon
Pete Daley—Elvin Tappe
Clay Dalrymple—Merritt Ranew
Mike Roarke—Jerry Zimmerman
Tom Satriano—Don Leppert
Phil Roof—Don Pavletich
Mike Brumley—Rene Lachemann

There are of course many others; the possibilities are in fact almost infinite. The game can be played with other positions too. First basemen (Lou Limmer—Elbie Fletcher), right fielders (Ron Northey—Dave Pope), and relief pitchers (George Zuverink—Hal Jeffcoat) were particularly fruitful areas for exploration. But catchers are really the best. I guess that's because there have been so many really lousy ones.

Charlie Lau was incidentally by no means the least talented of this mediocre mélange, although it was certainly not for want of trying. We just happened to latch onto his name because it possessed the proper vibrant timbre. Charlie actually holds the major league record for most doubles in one game—4. He set this record in 1962. It was downhill all the way from there.

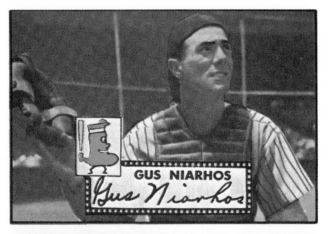

GUS NIARHOS

Gus Niarhos

"TOBY" ATWELL

catcher PITTSBURGH PIRATES

Toby Atwell

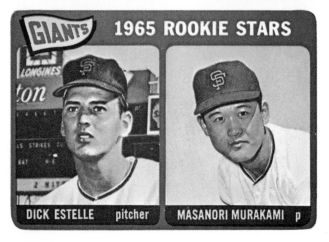

GIANTS 1965 ROOKIE STARS

DICK ESTELLE   pitcher

MASANORI MURAKAMI   p

But Gus Niarhos is really the guy that I think of when I get to reminiscing about terrible catchers. He was a weak-armed, slow-footed, poor-fielding backstop from Birmingham, Alabama, whose full legal name was Constantine Gregory Niarhos and who in nine major league seasons batted .252, drove in 59 runs and hit exactly one, yes one, home run. Gus was the sort of catcher who would have trouble making first string in most bullpens, although he looks ready for just about anything in this waxen 1951 image. Goes to show you how graphics can fool you. When Howie Pollett, the hard-throwing St. Louis left-hander, was asked how the Cardinals planned to pitch to Niarhos in an upcoming series with the Phillies, he replied, "We'll probably just throw him fast balls and bunch him toward the mound."

Toby Atwell has to be remembered by any serious collector of baseball cards in 1952 as having been one of the most difficult cards to acquire. He played for the Cubs that year, as pretty much their regular catcher, and later bounced around the National League as a second-string catcher for another five years before giving it up. But the career of Toby Atwell as player was secondary to the career of Toby Atwell as baseball card, and if you needed him to complete your set too, you'll know what I mean.

Masanori Murakami was, with the possible exception of Yogi Berra, the only man who ever played in the big leagues who did not speak English.

CLINT HARTUNG

Clint Hartung

Foster Castleman

3rd BASE   BALTIMORE ORIOLES

Clint Hartung, the "Hondo Hurricane" from Hondo, Texas, was a career New York Giant. He broke in as a pitcher and his 6'5", 210-pound size contributed to a baffling, if not wholly successful, pitching motion. What sets Cliff apart, however, was his switching to the outfield for the last two years of his career which, as you know, is equivalent in these days of specialized players to undergoing a heart transplant. Even though Cliff set no hitting records, he did prolong his career a year or two, and he got to play in the 1951 World Series, which I'm sure most of us would have been willing to undergo a heart transplant to do.

If, as Roger Price suggests, our names influence our personalities; if, that is, a man named Ulysses by his parents stands a better than even chance of becoming a general, or if, conversely, a boy christened Quasimodo is a very good bet to develop bad posture somewhere along the line, then there are definitely some names which should be avoided if you wish to steer your son in the direction of an athletic career. Might I suggest as an example that those contemplating the monikers Yehudi, Zachary, or Percy might better be advised to consider the alternate handles—Biff, Clete, or Bobby Joe—otherwise they run the risk of ending up with a fiddle player, an obscure President, or a poet with a bad cough. Believe me, if Sam Huff's name had been Wendell Narz he never would have gotten anywhere.

Which brings us to Foster Castleman.

Of course a ballplayer with a name like this is never going to amount to anything. If you have a name like an orthodontist you're going to play like an orthodontist. The guy never really had a shot. I mean where's the chance for a colorful nickname here? Foster "Night Train" Castleman? Foster "Big Daddy" Castleman? Not on your life. A center fielder named Wolfgang Amadeus DiMaggio stands about as much chance, in this least of all possible worlds, as a concert pianist named Peanuts Rubenstein. It's painfully obvious. If you want your kid to grow up to be a jock you can't call him something like Sinclair. Sinclair is either a right-wing Secretary of Commerce or a novelist with acne. If you take my advice you'll call the kid Brick. Nobody named Brick ever has to take anything from anybody.

On the other hand Duke Carmel had a perfect baseball name — brief, virile, alliterative. He just didn't have anything else to go along with it. This is a tragedy of a different order and one which I am not prepared to go into in great detail at this time, except to say that should you be considering a name such as Babe, Pee Wee, or Rocky for your firstborn son, it would perhaps be best to check out the little rascal's reflexes before you go about making it official.

Hal Griggs was to pitching as Wayne Causey was to hitting. That is to say — nothing. In four seasons with the Washington Senators from 1956 to 1959, Griggs had a record of 6-26 with an ERA of 5.50. He pitched 347 innings and gave up 392 hits. He walked 209 and struck out 172. He had one shutout.

Enough said.

Rip Repulski played his best years in the outfield for the Cardinals and the Phillies in the fifties. He followed Jabbo Jablonski in the batting order, and their names were always abbreviated in the box scores. On such things are nostalgic memories based.

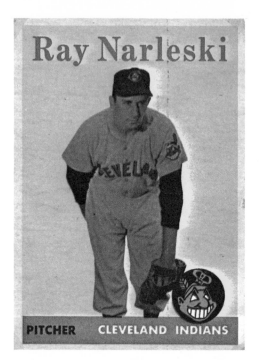

PITCHER   CLEVELAND INDIANS

Ideally every team in the majors should have at least two excellent relief pitchers — one left-handed and one right-handed. And ideally each of us should be handsome, charming, intelligent, and rich. Of course in the real world none of these things is ever going to come to pass, although for three brief years in the early fifties the Cleveland Indians had as close to the perfect relief tandem as any team is likely to come up with. Ray Narleski was the right-hander of the pair and Don Mossi the left-hander; and the efficiency of their work in the Indian bullpen was only overshadowed by their almost total lack of color and personality out of it. They always reminded me of two small-town undertakers who, having found the world at large a particularly cold and hardhearted place to do business in, have banded together in a desperate and distrustful partnership for the purposes of mutual self-preservation. Narleski with his sly little-boy grin and the darting, fishy eyes of the small-time criminal handles the customer relations, and Mossi with his loving-cup ears and the dark hulking presence of one newly dead or resurrected does all the dirty work. Eventually, of course, one of them hurt his arm and the other one was traded. This is the fate of all relief pitchers, their life expectancy being that of the average polliwog. I don't know what happened to either one of them after that, though. Like many another vapid couple of my acquaintance they did not seem to possess any separate identities and so soon vanished from sight like a distended and truncated amoeba.

DON MOSSI   pitcher

There are some ballplayers—Jimmy Foxx, Ty Cobb, and Sandy Amoros, for example—who seem truly lost when their playing days are over. They have trouble settling down, adjusting to their new lives, and even, occasionally, making a respectable living. Then there are other ex-big-leaguers like Joe Garagiola, Dominic DiMaggio, and Chuck Connors, whose playing careers seem only a coincidental prologue to their real careers. Joe Garagiola was a catcher for the Cardinals and the Pirates during the mid-fifties. We all know what he does now, of course, although I would find myself extremely hard-pressed were I required to define it. Suffice it to say that Joe was not nearly as inept a ballplayer as he has had the good sense to make himself out as, although he certainly could have been had he stayed at it long enough. He certainly had, as they say, all the tools.

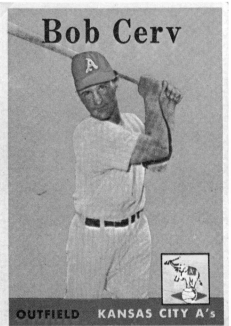

No, Bob Cerv is not trying to knock himself unconscious with a fungo bat.

And that is not a blue felt gravy boat he is wearing either.

Every player is required to have two pictures taken of him for his baseball card. One with, and one without, a baseball cap. Just in case, God forbid, he should be traded. This accounts for Bob Cerv's subtly counterfeited headgear in this picture, although it in no way accounts for his Yankee uniform.

Don't laugh. Somebody had to take five years of John Nagy art lessons to learn how to do airbrushing like that.

Some ballplayers have careers – Bob Feller, Wally Moses, Allie Reynolds, Walker Cooper. Some have years – Don Schwall, Luis Arroyo, Joe Christopher, Arnold Portocarrero. Still others have only minutes – Don Larsen, Bobby Thomson, Gene Bearden, Cookie Lavagetto. Charlie Maxwell was a little different from all of these; he had a series of days strung throughout a single year.

The day was Sunday.

And the year was 1956.

In 1956 Charlie Maxwell seemed to own Sundays. Every Sunday during the year I would turn on the radio to hear that Charlie Maxwell had hit 2 home runs, had gotten 8 hits in a doubleheader or had made a game-saving catch in the 13th inning. You just couldn't get Charlie out on Sundays. In fact all during that year Maxwell, who had never hit over .276 in his entire career, ended up with a lifetime batting average of .264, and all in all was the most undistinguished of undistinguishable second stringers, tore up the American League and terrorized its pitchers, hitting .326 with 28 home runs and 80 RBIs and made the American League All Star team as a starter. He was 29 years old and was in his sixth major league season. During the preceeding five years he had hit a total of 10 home runs, had 35 RBIs, 71 hits and a lifetime batting average of .222. It only lasted one year though, and by 1959 Charlie was back hitting in the mid .250's, was no problem to any pitcher of any description, not even on Sundays, and was well on his way back to the well-earned and full-time obscurity which he so clearly coveted. And nobody, least of all Charlie, has ever been able to figure out what happened in 1956.

CHARLEY
MAXWELL
CHICAGO WHITE SOX   OF

Ernie Banks, "Mr. Cub," needs no introduction. He was one of those great players who was cursed to play out his career with an inferior team. It is no exaggeration to say that the difference between an Ernie Banks and a Mickey Mantle is the good fortune to play with a championship team. Ernie Banks never had that good fortune. Still, there was something about him that even opponents' fans applauded.

Stan Musial, as we all know, was one of the best players of all time, a first-rate hitter and a perennial batting champion. But what might get overlooked in a recounting of Stan the Man's accomplishments on the field is the memory of why there was no card of him issued in 1950 and 1951. Does anybody know for sure? It was something that all collectors talked about at the time—how could you play a game with baseball cards using the Cardinals without Musial? You got tired of saying that he was injured, when in fact he had the reputation of being an iron man who played every game, and who was too valuable to be out of the lineup. If anyone knows why there were no cards of Stan during those years, please write to the authors in care of their publisher.

In 1957 a nationwide television audience was treated to the highly irregular but singularly entertaining spectacle of a terrified New York Giant starting pitcher, in the person of Ruben Gomez, being chased hell bent for leather around the grassy perimeters of the Milwaukee Brave infield by an enraged bat-wielding assailant. The fact that the incensed protagonist resembled to an astounding degree the Braves' dour, gorillalike first baseman, Joe Adcock, no doubt accounts to a great extent for the markedly impetuous character of Mr. Gomez's retreat, Adcock being just a shade or two less terrifying in countenance than the Cookie Monster.

There have been many other incidents of counterbrushback or antibean throughout the long tempestuous history of major league baseball, but none up until this point that was quite so noticeably pregnant with the unmistakable aura of physical mayhem. Mr. Gomez was rumored to have been so unnerved by this incident in fact that he was unable to pitch in Milwaukee for the rest of the year, and there are those close to the Giant situation who insist that after his little enforced jaunt around the base paths Ruben was never quite the same again.

Of course considering what he was like in the first place that is not necessarily all that bad.

In addition to looking like every clean-cut, square-shooting, Sunday School-attending, devoted to his family, straight A student and Eagle Scout who ever took an ax to his grandmother, Don Buddin had one other cross to bear during his brief and disastrous major league tenure.

He was a professional goat.

Now your professional goats come in all sizes, shapes and dispositions. There is your small-time goat like Elio Chacon, a moderately gifted shortstop for the Reds and the Mets in the early sixties, who could never seem to do anything quite right. There is your big-time goat like Ozzie Virgil, an itinerant utility infielder of blessed memory whose entire big league career was characterized by a pristine and diamond-hard propensity for mishandling the basics. There are your part-time goats like Ralph Branca or Mickey Cochrane, admirable athletes whose otherwise distinguished careers were marred by a single catastrophic happenstance the notoriety of which will live on long after them. And there is your full-time goat like Lu Clinton, who was so bad that I don't even want to go into it.

Don Buddin was a little different from all these.

For Don Buddin was a creative goat.

He was the sort of guy who would perform admirably, even flawlessly, for seven or eight innings of a ball game, or until such time as you really needed him. Then he would promptly fold like Dick Contino's accordion. Choke. Explode. Disintegrate. Like a cheap watch or a '54 Chevy. He would give up the ghost and depart. Don Buddin would make 40 errors a year and 38 of them would lose ball games. He would get 130 hits during a season, only 6 of which would come with men on. He would neglect to touch a base during a rally, lose pop-ups in the sun in extra innings, forget the count and try to bunt with 2 strikes. If there was a way to make the worst out of a situation, Don Buddin could be counted on to find it. There is a little bit of this in many of us, of course, and quite a bit of it in fact in most, but then again we aren't being paid big league salaries are we, or being interviewed by "Collier's" magazine?

Who the hell is Cuno Barragan? And why are they saying those terrible things about him?

Just as the fifties was a bad decade for rock and roll singers traveling in private airplanes—Buddy Holly, Richie Valens, the Big Bopper—so was the sixties a bad decade for professional athletes traveling in private airplanes—Rocky Marciano, Tony Lema, Rafael Ossuna.

Kenny Hubbs was an extremely promising young second baseman with the Chicago Cubs, .287 batting average in 1964, rookie of the year at twenty-two. He was killed in the crash of a private plane over Provo, Utah, on February 23, 1965.

We still remember you Kenny.

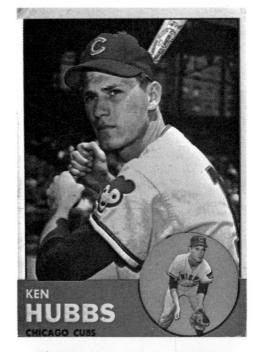

The nicest thing that Topps could figure out to say about Eddie Miksis was that he was tenth in the National League in stolen bases in 1951, with 11. Hardly an earthquaking statistic after seven years in the majors. He had a lifetime batting average of .236 and 44 career home runs. Miksis was the sort of guy that if you were introduced to him at a party and he told you he was a big league ballplayer, you'd think he was kidding.

In a way he would have been.

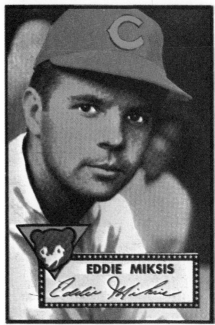

Vern Law was one of several deeply religious men to play in organized baseball. He was called "Deacon," and was in fact a deacon. He pitched for the Pirates for sixteen seasons, and was one of the primary reasons that the team won the pennant and the World Series in 1960. Does anyone remember the names of his wife and his several children? They all started with the letter "V," and they were all of biblical significance. Anyone who remembers something like that, and who is not a lifelong Pirates' fan, should be awarded a prize of some sort.

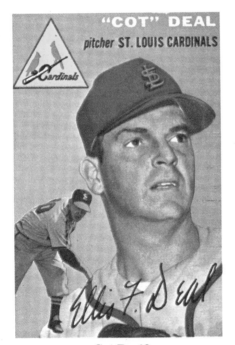

Cot Deal?

Granny Hamner was one of the all-time Philadelphia Phillie greats. He played shortstop for fifteen years with that team, and he was the only bright spot in the Whiz Kid 1950 World Series against the Yankees, going 6-for-14 and sparking the few rallies the Phillies started. Granny was the type of player you take for granted because he just about always came through. Not the most exciting guy, you might say, but the kind of player you remember twenty years later, in a positive way, as having defined a team's spirit.

Bill Nicholson was nicknamed "Swish" somewhat cruelly, and not for the reason you're probably thinking. Swish did one of two things when he came to bat: either he struck out or he hit a home run. There was no middle ground. He led the National League in the early forties in RBI's (twice), and in home runs (also twice). He was always, even in his last years with the Phillies as a pinch-hitter, a long ball threat. It was imperative that he hit home runs as he got older, though, because it was questionable whether he could get around the bases in any kind of hurry with all of the weight he carried then.

Larry Doby was the first black player in the American League, which is a little like being the second person to invent the telephone. This plus the fact that he was not as colorful or as talented as Jackie Robinson and that he spent most of his major league career toiling in the torpid atmosphere of Cleveland's Municipal Stadium accounts to a great measure for his singular lack of notoriety. He was a good ballplayer though, and along with Al Rosen, Jim Hegan, and Gene Woodling backboned the offensive side of those excellent Indian teams in the mid-fifties. He was the right man all right—but certainly not in the right time or place.

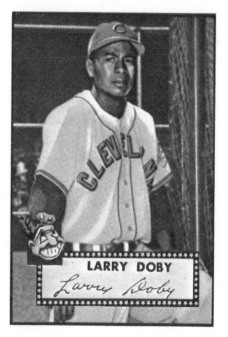

SERIES HURLING RIVALS
LOU BURDETTE • BOBBY SHANTZ

YANKS CELEBRATE
AS TERRY WINS

WORLD
SERIES
GAME
#7

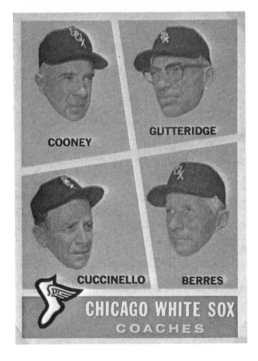

COONEY

GUTTERIDGE

CUCCINELLO

BERRES

CHICAGO WHITE SOX
COACHES

To fill out a series for collectors and to provide a change of pace for the rest of us, the card companies would occasionally issue special cards—about twenty-five or thirty a year. Coach cards. Rookie cards. Historical cards. Cards with highlights of last year's World Series. Manager cards. Star cards. Record cards. As well as the inevitable and much-dreaded series checklists.

The cards were all right in themselves. But they were nothing in comparison with their headlines: Sluggers Supreme (Kluszewski and Williams). Rival Fence Busters (Mays and Snider). Pitchers Beware! Cubs Clouters. Destruction Crew. Pitching Partners. Batter Bafflers. Words of Wisdom. Keystone Combo. Power Plus. Heavy Artillery. Bombers Best. Giant Gunners. Tribe Hill Trio.

The composer of these little captions believed in alliteration, and wasn't the least bit bashful about laying it on—Master and Mentor. Soph Stalwarts. Mound Magicians. Cincy Clouters. Beantown Bombers. Card Clubbers. Tribe Thumpers. Mets Maulers. Bengal Belters. Twin Terrors. Astro Aces. Tiger Twirlers.

But my favorites were the particularly enigmatic items—Lindy Shows Larry. Bill's Got It. Corsair Trio. They always looked so intriguing on a checklist. I mean what could they possibly be?

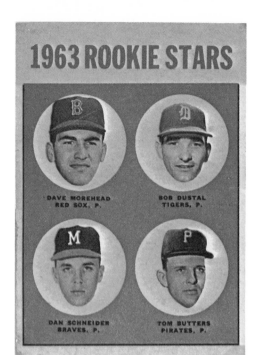

1963 ROOKIE STARS

DAVE MOREHEAD
RED SOX, P.

BOB DUSTAL
TIGERS, P.

DAN SCHNEIDER
BRAVES, P.

TOM BUTTERS
PIRATES, P.

BROOKLYN—BOSTON
PLAY 26-INNING TIE

CASEY TEACHES

CASEY STENGEL • ED KRANEPOOL

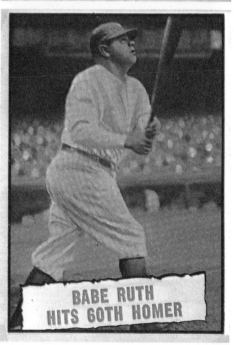

BABE RUTH
HITS 60TH HOMER

RIVAL FENCE BUSTERS
WILLIE MAYS • DUKE SNIDER

On the theory that there is no ballplayer so obscure that there won't be somebody around who can remember him we take great pride in presenting Paul Smith. The back of his card informs us that he simply cannot miss as a Pirate outfielder (or flycatcher) next year. So what happened? Frankly I never heard of the guy but I can tell you one thing — if he doesn't stop swinging the bat that way, he's going to break both his arms.

PITTSBURGH PIRATES OUTFIELD

Roy Face started only 24 games in fifteen years of major league pitching, mostly with the Pirates. He appeared, however, in 804 games. He was perhaps the most effective career relief pitcher baseball has ever known. He achieved a phenomenal 18-1 record in 1959. Roy was one of those players managers love to have on their rosters: he was always there, ready to step in when things got rough — which, for the Pirates (with the exception of the 1960 season), was frequently. He perfected a pitch known as the "palm ball," which behaved oddly and unpredictably on its course toward the plate, but which usually got over the plate, and got batters to swing unsuccessfully at it, and — what's worse — to worry about it to distraction.

Joey Jay was, as far as I know, the first major leaguer to be called a bonus baby, and the only one to be so called throughout his entire career. He looked like a bonus baby. The extra money Milwaukee paid him was to no avail for at least eight years, by which time he was pitching for Cincinnati anyway, where he threw 21–10 and 21–14 seasons back-to-back, with a few of those victories against the Braves, to confirm their foresightedness in giving him that bonus.

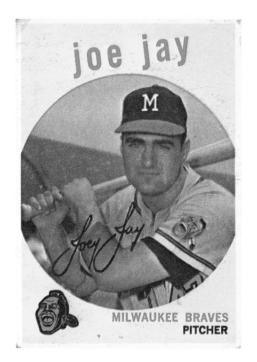

The most impressive personal record in baseball history is the 56-game consecutive-hitting streak of Joe DiMaggio. The second most impressive personal record in baseball history is the winning of 20 games by Ned Garver with the 1951 St. Louis Browns. In recording this feat, which must rank in terms of sheer miraculousness somewhere in between Johnny Vander Meer's consecutive no-hitters and the raising of Lazarus, Garver became the first pitcher since 1924 to win 20 games with a last-place ball club. And he only lost 12. In fact those 20 victories were 38 percent of the entire Browns' total for that year.

Now when a good hitter is with a bad ball club he's basically all right. If he is at all competitive then all the losing might get to him and he'll probably be a bit short in the RBIs and runs scored, but still he's going to get his hits and everybody will know what he's worth. But a good pitcher with a bad ball club is just plain screwed. Nobody scores any runs for him, nobody makes the big hit. The outfielders kill him with errors and the infielders lack any kind of range. The management is bitter and insulting. The crowds are sparse and often hostile. Even his friends are likely to turn against him. He is surrounded by ineptitude and indifference. Discourtesy and discouragement fill his days. And nobody ever does anything to try and shore up his morale. He is like Sviatoslav Richter playing with a Salvation Army band. There is no telling how good Garver might have been with a good club but after five or six years with the Brownies, whom their owner Bill Veeck has often referred to as the worst team in the history of major league baseball, he wasn't much good for anything. The last time I saw him his right arm was about two inches shorter than his left, he looked like he was going to pass out every time he threw a slider, and he wasn't throwing hard enough to break a soft boiled egg against Willy Tasby's skull.

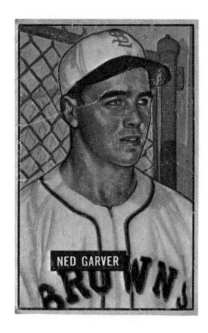

What would baseball be without nicknames?

"American Bandstand" without Kenny Rossi?

A suburban tract house without a bomb shelter?

A new toothpaste without hexachlorophene or chlorophyll?

The players of the fifties had their share of colorful nicknames. Some of them even made sense.

Whitey Lockman had white hair indeed. Pee Wee Reese was a former marbles champion. Birdie Tebbetts had a voice like a sparrow. Charles Dillon Stengel came from K. C. (Missouri).

Mike Garcia really was a big bear. Sam McDowell's deliveries were assuredly sudden. Johnny Hopp couldn't help but be Hippity. Virgil Trucks was inevitably Fire.

But Ducky Schofield? Possum Burright? Footsie Belardi? Honey Romano? Moonman Shannon? Hurricane Hazle?

How are we to account for these deprecating handles? Can calling a grown man Ducky or Footsie possibly be justified?

To say nothing of Symphony Ciaffone. Or Ding-a-Ling Clay. Or Tomato Face Lamabe.

And then there was Frank House who was known as The Pig. And Elijah Green whose teammates called him Pumpsie.

The following three players had equally interesting nicknames. And even more interesting ways of living up to them:

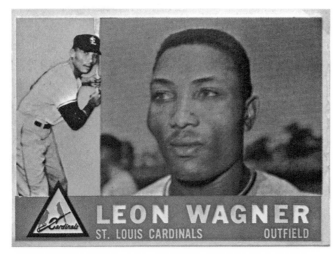

Leon Wagner was known as Daddy Wags. If you don't know why then you weren't paying attention.

Dick Stuart could fill a book by himself. Being the legitimate cookoo king of the era. He hit 66 home runs one year in the minors and campaigned vigorously each season for the All Star team. He had a television show in each city that he played in and was the first American star to play in Japan. He refused to bunt no matter what the situation and seemed to endorse any product that would pay him fifty bucks. He never stopped talking during his entire career and carried on feuds with almost everyone but the ushers. He might not have been the greatest natural eccentric of the decade but he definitely got the most out of what he had to work with. It was his inability to field his position, however, that gained him his string of unflattering nicknames—"Stonefingers," "The Boston Strangler," "Doctor Strangeglove." Highly insulting but all richly deserved. Dick Stuart's fielding had to be seen to be believed. He charted new dimensions in defensive ineptitude. He dropped foul pop-ups, misplayed grounders, bobbled bunts. He missed pick-off throws, dropped relays, messed up force plays. He fell down while covering the bag on easy rollers, knocked his teammates down while circling under flies. Every ball hit his way was an adventure, the most routine play a fresh challenge to his artlessness. It is hard to describe this to anyone who has not seen it. Just as it is hard to describe Xavier Cugat or Allan Ludden.

Stu once picked up a hot dog wrapper that was blowing toward his first base position. He received a standing ovation from the crowd. It was the first thing he had managed to pick up all day, and the fans realized that it could very well be the last.

DICK
STUART
BOSTON RED SOX 1B

Ken Harrelson was referred to affectionately as The Hawk. A check of his profile will supply you with the reason. Harrelson introduced long hair and outrageous attitudes to the Sporting World. He was the first of the Athletic Free Spirits. He was also the only one of these self-indulgent postadolescents with enough presence to carry it off. Derek Sanderson and Duane Thomas please note.

OUTFIELD
RED SOX
KEN HARRELSON

The following is a list of major league nicknames. If you don't believe me, so help me, you can look them up.

Wagon Tongue
  Adams
Snitz Applegate
Bow Wow Arft
Bee Bee Babe
Rattlesnake Baker
Desperate Beatty
Bananas Benes
Jittery Joe Berry
Hill Billy Bildilli
The Darling Booth
Goobers Bratcher
Chops Broskie
Turkeyfoot Brower
Scoops Carey
Ding-a-Ling Clay
Whoops Creeden
Crunchy Cronin
Dingle Croucher
Daffy Dean
Peaceful Valley
  Deizer
Hickory Dickson
Bullfrog Dietrich
Buttermilk Dowd
Pea Soup Dumont
Piccolo Pete Elko
Slippery Ellam
Broadway Flair
Sleuth Fleming
Suds Fodge
Inch Gleich
Gabber Glenn
Snags Heidrick
Bunny High
Bootnose Hofmann
Herky Jerky Horton
Twinkles Host
Highpockets Hunt
Bear Tracks Javery
Grasshopper Lillie

Whoop-La White
Swamp Baby Wilson
Bunions Zeider
Goober Zuber
Ethan Allen
Sweetbreads Bailey

Humpy McElveen
Sadie McMahon
Boob McNair
Spinach Melillo
Earache Meyer
Peach Pie O'Connor
Primo Preibisch
Truckhorse Pratt
Lumber Price
Shucks Pruett
Raw Meat Rodgers
Half-Pint Rye
Horse Belly Sargent
Silk Stocking Schafer
Steeple Schultz
Blab Schwartz
Twinkletoes Selkirk
Spook Speake
Fish Hook Stout
Candy LaChance
Bevo LeBourveau
Razor Ledbetter
Memo Luna
Cuddles Marshall
Beauty McGowan
Charlie Nice
Orval Overall
Pretzels Pezzullo
Clarence Pickrel
Ty Pickup
Wally Pipp
Cotton Pippen
Pinky Pittenger
Arlie Pond
Elmer Ponder
Pid Purdy
Shadow Pyle
Wimpy Quinn
Icicle Reeder
Tink Riviere
Slim Sallee

Lady Baldwin
Cuke Barrows
Belve Bean
Boom-Boom Beck
Boze Berger
Red Bird

Skeeter Scalzi
Wildfire Schulte
Pius Scwert
Bob Seeds
Socks Seibold
Mule Shirley
Ivey Shiver
Urban Shocker
Colonel Bosco Snyder
Inky Strange
Sleeper Sullivan
Homer Summa
Suds Sutherland
Ducky Swann
Patsy Tebeau
Pussy Tebeau
White Wings Tebeau
Adonis Terry
Ben Tincup
Cannonball Titcomb
Tommy Tucker
Turkey Tyson
Dixie Upright
Dike Varney
Peak-a-Boo Veach
Jake Virtue
Fleet Walker
Mysterious Walker
George Washington
Mother Watson
Mule Watson
Stump Weidman
Podgie Weihe
Icehouse Wilson
Kettle Wirtz
Chicken Wolf
Yam Yaryan
Chief Moses
  Yellowhorse
Zip Zabel
Noodles Zupo
Bruno Block
Joe Blong
Lu Blue
Ossie Bluege
Bunny Brief
Oyster Burns

Pumpsie Green was the first black player on the Boston Red Sox, the last team to admit a black player to its major league roster. In 1959 irate fans paraded around Fenway Park for three days protesting the Red Sox refusal to bring Pumpsie up from the minors. When he was finally brought up in the middle of the year, he disappointed even his most ardent supporters by being unable to either hit major league pitching or field major league hitting, thus achieving immediate and total equality with the rest of the Red Sox lineup. He disappointed no one, however, with his bizarre behavior. One summer weekend in 1962, when after a particularly humiliating defeat at the hands of the New York Yankees, he and Gene Conley, the erratic 6'8" basketball-playing pitcher, walked off the team bus in the middle of a traffic jam in the Bronx and disappeared into the postgame crowd. They were not encountered again until nearly three days later, when an alert "New York Post" sports reporter spotted them standing in line at Idlewild International Airport attempting to board a plane for Israel—with no luggage, no passport, and in what in all candor must be described as a markedly inebriated condition. Needless to say, they did not make it onto the plane. No explanation was ever given for their behavior. Green was returned to Louisville shortly thereafter. Conley was given his release at the beginning of the next season.

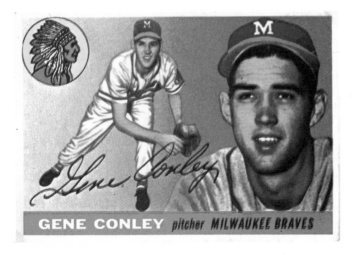

Funny, he doesn't look Jewish.

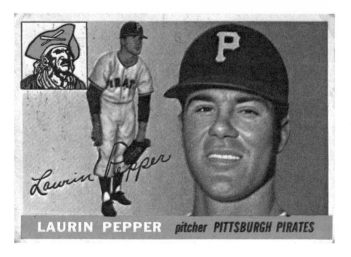

LAURIN PEPPER   *pitcher* PITTSBURGH PIRATES

Laurin Pepper was offered contracts by both the Pirates and the football Steelers upon his graduation from college, and ol' Laurin, from Vaughan, Mississippi, made the wrong choice by signing with the Pirates. He couldn't have helped but do better playing football. Over the course of four seasons he won 2 and lost 8, and ran up an ERA of 7.06, which has to be a record of some sort. The bonus he received from the Pirates back in the early fifties is probably still paying his rent back in Vaughan.

Joe Nuxhall was perhaps most famous for breaking in with Cincinnati in 1944 at the tender age of sixteen, pitching two-thirds of one inning, giving up two hits and walking five. After that game, Joe retired voluntarily, and wasn't seen again in the majors until 1952. But from that point, Joe just went on and on, finally giving up in 1966 when he injured his arm, still pitching for Cincinnati. One had the feeling that had he not been forced to retire early, Joe might have outlasted Satchel Paige as the oldest pitcher in baseball.

JIM GILLIAM   2nd base BROOKLYN DODGERS

Junior Gilliam stepped in at second base in his rookie season with the Brooklyn Dodgers, 1953, when that team was in its prime, or maybe just passing it. His exceptional speed turned doubles into triples, and he led the league in triples his first year. He was always among the stolen-base leaders, and was agile and effective as an infielder over the course of a 14-year career.

Quick, name a major league baseball player who was born in San Reno, Italy, lived in Windsor, Ontario, Canada, and couldn't hit.

That's right—Reno Bertoia.

OK. Name another one.

The back of Reno's card is interesting. It says that his average last year was .162 and that, although he did not get to play in too many ball games, he gained valuable information about American League hurlers that would help him in the future. I suspect that the information he gathered was that every pitcher in the American League could get him out, and that perhaps he should try some other line of work.

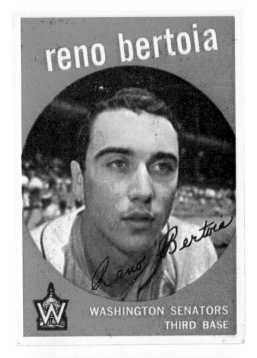

Del Ennis was the kind of slugger every successful team seems to have. When Del came to bat, no matter what the situation, the crowd came alive. The promise of the long ball, the game-breaking home run, was always there. His 31 homers led the Phillies in their pennant year but he slumped badly in the World Series, going 2-for-14 as his team was swept by the Yankees.

Is there anyone who doesn't know that Ralph Branca threw Bobby Thomson the home run ball that won the pennant for the Giants and lost it for the Dodgers in 1951? It is curious how a chance, two-minute encounter on a motley overgrown playing field in the hazy late September sun can wed two men more or less permanently in the collective consciousness of a nation. It is further curious that Thomson, a mediocre outfielder at best throughout his entire major league career, should emerge the hero of this encounter, and Branca, an excellent pitcher for the Dodgers for many years, the goat. But no matter what these two might have accomplished before or since, that is all anybody is ever going to remember them for. I have it on good authority, incidentally, that Branca, who took his misfortune particularly hard at the time — as who among us would not — is now rather happy that the whole thing transpired, as it affords him the opportunity to demand exorbitant speaking fees at numerous public functions in and around the greater New York area.

I doubt it.

CAN'T ANYBODY HERE PLAY THIS GAME?

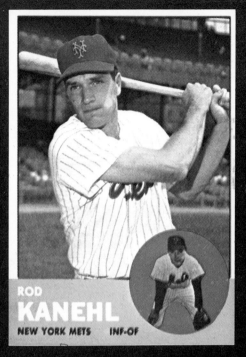

ROD
KANEHL
NEW YORK METS   INF-OF

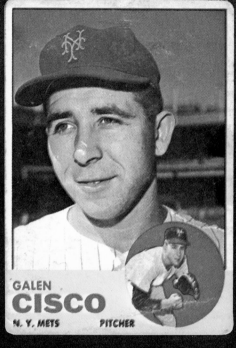

GALEN
CISCO
N. Y. METS   PITCHER

The 1962 New York Mets had a record of 40 wins and 120 losses.
   Their best pitcher was Al Jackson with an ERA of 4.40. Their utility in-fielder, Rod Kanehl, made 32 errors. They had records of 2-16 against both Los Angeles and Pittsburgh. Their best hitter, Richie Ashburn, was thirty-five years old. Their manager, Casey Stengel, frequently fell asleep on the bench.

NEW YORK METS

Sandy Amoros was a member of the second-to-last generation of excellent black ballplayers exported to the United States from Cuba after the end of the Second World War. He was a speedy, heady, solid outfielder, who helped anchor the numerous Dodger pennant winners of the fifties and early sixties. He made front-page headlines in 1956 when his spectacular catch of a Yogi Berra line drive helped win the World Series for Brooklyn and, again in 1970, when he was discovered penniless and unemployed, applying for family assistance in an upper Manhattan welfare office. This is an indication of how far the mighty can fall in this country if they are black, unskilled, not particularly thrifty, come from Cuba, or have at one time or another worked for Walter O'Malley.

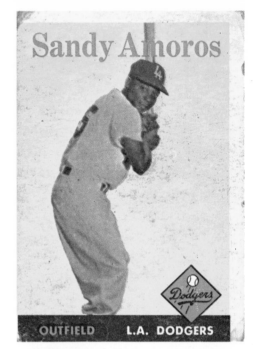

Elmer Valo was a journeyman outfielder who managed to stay in the majors for twenty years. He was an average hitter, but an exceptional pinch hitter, particularly in his later years. What I will always remember Elmer Valo for, however, will be his spectacular catches in deep left field in Philadelphia's Connie Mack Stadium, catches that inevitably had him crashing into the wall and crumpling dazed to the ground, with his glove in the air and the ball still in it.

Stan Lopata was a good, big catcher with the Phillies, who hit out of a peculiar crouching stance that presented a very difficult target for a pitcher because it effectively reduced the strike zone. As much as pitchers complained to umpires about Stan's stance being illegal, however, the stance didn't do Stan that much good, except maybe in 1956, when he hit 32 homers and 33 doubles.

It is hard to pin down the exact birthdate of the bonus-baby syndrome, that fascinating brainchild of the athletic free enterprise system, but it was unquestionably during the late fifties and early sixties that it finally reached the dazzling and dizzying heights of overinflated economic absurdity. Johnny Antonelli was an early product of this era of extravagance. The Braves paid 65 Gs for young Mr. Antonelli's John Hancock on a standard National League contract in 1948 and were rewarded for their generosity with records of 2-3 in 1949, 6-9 in 1950, and 5-8 in 1953. Convinced of the error of their ways, they finally shipped him off to the New York Giants in 1954, where he proceeded to win 26 games, a pennant, and a world championship for Horace Stoneham. The Boston teams specialized in capers like this. The Red Sox once paid a $40,000 bonus to a markedly mediocre Boston area black outfielder in a shameless attempt to indicate the sincerity of their decidedly insincere intentions of employing athletes of the colored persuasion. They also once gifted a free-swinging sandlot first baseman from Jamaica Plain, named Bobby Guindon, with a $125,000 bonus, even though my friend Bob Hines had once struck him out three times in a game against Boston English High School and reported to me afterward that it was common knowledge that Guindon could not, even at that juncture, get within six inches of any halfway decent breaking pitch.

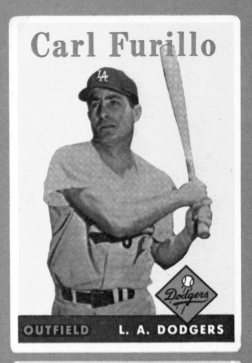

Carl Furillo

OUTFIELD · L. A. DODGERS

I
See
the
Boys
of
Summer
in their
Ruin
Lay
the
Golden
Tithings
Barren

Billy Cox

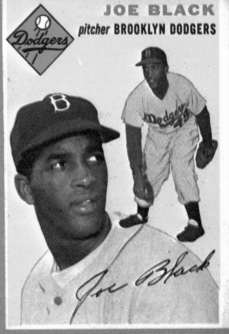

JOE BLACK
pitcher BROOKLYN DODGERS

Joe Black

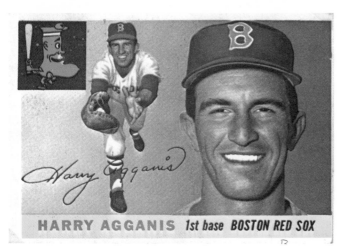

HARRY AGGANIS 1st base BOSTON RED SOX

The Golden Greek. An All American quarterback at Boston University, a fancy fielding, home-run hitting first baseman for the Boston Red Sox, a tall, handsome, clean-cut son of immigrant parents, a good student, an all-around athlete, a youth leader and a teen-age idol, Harry Agganis was the epitome of the American dream. The day that he died of leukemia at age 25, in 1955, I was attending a performance of the Big Brother Bob Emery television program with a group of my fellow Cub Scouts. I can still remember the oversized headlines in the Boston newspapers and the feeling of stunned incredulity they aroused in all of us—our first encounter with the underlying frailty of the human condition. Up until then death had been something that only happened to animals or in the movies or to bank robbers or people who had fires in their houses or to the old. But Harry Agganis? If something like this could happen to Harry Agganis then what was to become of us?

What indeed?

Eddie Gaedel was the midget whom Bill Veeck put up to pinch hit in a game against the Tigers in 1952. As is the case with most midgets, he did not have a particularly large strike zone, so that he was able to walk on four straight pitches. I would like to be able to report that Little Eddie, as I call him, upon reaching first base immediately set off in a valiant if ill-advised attempt to steal second, and that while his tiny midget-like legs were carrying him along the basepaths, the Browns left town on an extended road trip, but I'm afraid I would be straining your credulity just a bit with this particular anecdote. The plain ugly facts of the matter are that the diminutive batsman was lifted almost immediately for a pinch runner and that one week later he was ruled out of baseball forever by Commissioner William Harridge, a hard-hearted and humorless man with a highly underdeveloped sense of the appropriate. Gaedel is listed in the "Baseball Encyclopedia" as a left-hand-hitting, right-hand-throwing outfielder, standing 3'7" and weighing 85 pounds. He passed away in 1963, perhaps of a broken heart or, as seems even more appropriate, by simply growing smaller and smaller until he finally disappeared.

Whitey Herzog caught the ball that was thrown out by President Eisenhower to open the major league season in 1958. This may not seem like much to you but, believe me, it was definitely the highlight of Whitey's career.

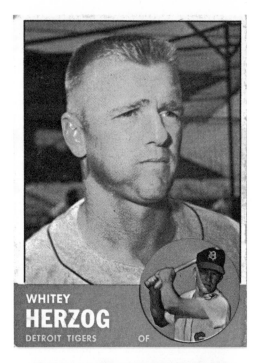

WHITEY
HERZOG
DETROIT TIGERS   OF

Early Wynn. I remember going to see the Philadelphia Athletics play the Cleveland Indians one night in 1952, and the game was billed as the pitching duel of the year; Early Wynn against Bobby Shantz. Wynn won 23 games that year, Shantz 24 to lead the league. It was a fine game, won by Cleveland 2-1, and the focus of the game, all the way through, was on the pitching. When that happens, when the fans hang on every pitch, even the batters seem intimidated. Wynn and Shantz, but especially Wynn, pitched almost flawlessly. Although Wynn was plagued by injuries throughout his career, he remained one of the top pitchers in the American League, with one of the most complete books ever seen on the batters he faced.

JOHNNY LIPON

Ewell Blackwell was nicknamed "The Whip" in tribute to his side-arm pitching motion. Just as he brought his arm back, immediately before whipping it forward and releasing the ball toward the plate, he kind of cocked his arm, much in the same way as you might cock your arm before snapping a whip. He stood 6'6" and was painfully thin, and all of this was quite dazzling to batters. His lifetime record, over the course of ten years, was a winning one, and he led the National League in strike-outs in 1947 with 193, the same year he went 22-8, with 23 complete games.

Andy Seminick was the hardrock, fireplug catcher for the Whiz Kid Phillies. He was the one who directed—and catchers too rarely get credit for this—Robin Roberts, Curt Simmons, and the reliever Jim Konstanty to their best seasons. He caught almost every game, and hit a strong .288, with 24 home runs.

Johnny Lipon and Dick Brodowski should never, under any circumstances, have been allowed out of the house without their mothers.

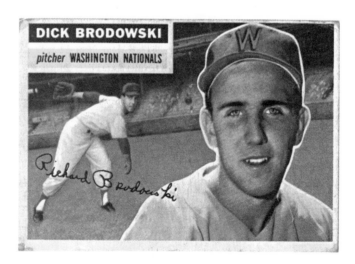

HERB SCORE
pitcher CLEVELAND INDIANS

Sometimes it is a bit difficult to figure out just what is going on in the background of a particular baseball card. Pitchers are shown sliding into third base, catchers are shown scratching their armpits, coaches assume particularly meaningless expressions. It is all very disconcerting and enigmatic. From all that I can surmise about this particular glossy of Al Silvera, a collegiate outfielder with Cincinnati in the mid-fifties who, despite Topps' prediction for him of eminent stardom, never managed to play a full season in the majors—he is either performing some sort of baroque Sicilian fertility dance or preparing to catch a bag of chicken salad sandwiches from the press box.

AL SILVERA
outfield CINCINNATI REDLEGS

There are those who covet death.

And there are those whom death covets.

On August 17, 1920, Ray Chapman of the Cleveland Indians and Beaver Dam, Kentucky, was struck in the head and killed by a pitched ball thrown by Ray Mays of the New York Yankees and Liberty, Kentucky, thus becoming the only man ever to be killed during the playing of a major league baseball game.

On August 3, 1940, Willard Hershberger, the wiry, injury-prone second-string catcher of the Cincinnati Reds, distraught over what he considered his negative contribution to a lengthy Reds' losing streak, took his own life by means of hanging, in room 306B of the Miles Standish Hotel in downtown Boston, Massachusetts, thus becoming the only major league baseball player ever to commit suicide during the course of a regular season.

And on May 6, 1957, Herb Score, an overpoweringly fast left-handed pitcher for the Cleveland Indians from Rosedale, New York, had his extremely promising career prematurely and permanently terminated when a line drive from the bat of Gil McDougald, the aging New York Yankee shortstop from San Francisco, California, hit him squarely and forcefully under the left eye, knocking him unconscious and temporarily blinding him.

There are all kinds of death, just as there are all kinds of life.

Some are quick and some are slow.

Some are happy and some are sad.

Some are easy. Some are not.

One summer when I was about twelve years old and not particularly wise, as I am today (God help me) in the ways of the world, some supermarket chain or other in the greater Boston area ran a promotion wherein they invited prospective customers to come in and meet a couple of the less luminous lights in the lavish Red Sox galaxy in the friendly, unhurried atmosphere of the Saturday morning checkout counter—somewhere in between the chocolate-covered fish cakes and the curried bananas. When I arrived on the scene with my friends, Tony Werra and Steve Gladdis, hot, dirty, and exhausted after a six-mile walk in 90° heat, we were informed that only those privileged members of the consuming public who were prepared to pop for five skins worth of Cocoa Puffs, Ex-Lax, Mallomars, and Barcolean were entitled to enter the premises, peruse the assembled dignitaries, and hustle an autograph or two.

In other words—no kids.

I carry three memories of that day to the present.

First is the vivid recollection of our long, discouraging walk home through the grimy summertime haze of North Dorchester.

Second is the image of little Billy Klaus, the Red Sox scrappy second baseman, sitting somewhere in the vicinity of the cash register, his $65 hand-sewn Gucci loafers propped up on a stack of strawberry Yoo-Hoo, gazing out through the Thermopane at the assembled hordes of unwelcome children with what can only be described as a benevolently malicious grin.

And third is a dislike, bordering on disgust, for the commercial proclivities of well-known athletes such as Bobby Hull, Tom Seaver, and Walt Frazier, who, it has often seemed to me, would be sorely tempted to shill diseased blankets to the Indians if they thought there was a buck in it for them.

BILLY
KLAUS
PHILA. PHILLIES   INF.

ALBIE
PEARSON
LOS ANGELES ANGELS   OF

Albie Pearson would have been, had he been only six inches taller, almost 5'11".

Here he is standing next to his favorite bat, Merle.

Eddie Waitkus, from Cambridge, Massachusetts, made the front pages in 1949 when he was shot by a jealous girlfriend in a hotel room in St. Louis. This incident, and the fact that Eddie was a graceful, effective first baseman and a steady hitter with the Phillies in their glory years, provided the inspiration for one of Bernard Malamud's best novels, "The Natural." Eddie died in mid-1972, before his time, as they say; and a low-keyed, tragic life played itself out.

If the camera indeed does not lie then what are we to make of all this.

Tex Clevenger could never seem to shake the lingering and nagging self-doubt which plagued him throughout his career. Given his record, of course, this was readily understandable. But couldn't he have tried a little harder to cover it up? In this picture he seems to be saying to himself, "Geez, maybe I should get out of this racket."

Geez Tex, maybe you should.

But in the meantime stop picking your fingernails.

Rollie Sheldon, Johnny Kucks, Duke Maas, Jim Coates, Hal Reniff, Fred Talbot, and Dooley Womack to the contrary, you knew the Yankee pitching staff had really hit rock bottom when Eli Grba managed to slither his way into the starting rotation. In addition to having the hardest name to pronounce in the big leagues he also had just about the worst stuff. This is not an easy combination for any manager to bear and so Eli was cut adrift in the first expansion draft to the Los Angeles Angels. Here he joined Ted Bowsfield, Ron Kline, Ryne Duren, and Art Fowler to make up what must have been the most totally and unredeemedly washed up pitching staff of all time.

ELI GRBA
Pitcher

Los Angeles Angels

Johnny Logan was nicknamed "Yatcha" for some reason that no one can fathom, but in spite of that, he was a consistently good shortstop for the Braves in the fifties. He was the kind of player who could spark rallies in the late innings, and was always the first player on the mound to encourage his pitcher when things got rough. With all his leadership abilities, I'm sure he must be a manager of some minor league team now, or at least sales manager for a prepared foods company.

JOHNNY LOGAN
Shortstop

Milwaukee Braves

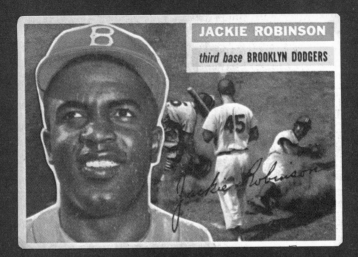

JACKIE ROBINSON
third base BROOKLYN DODGERS

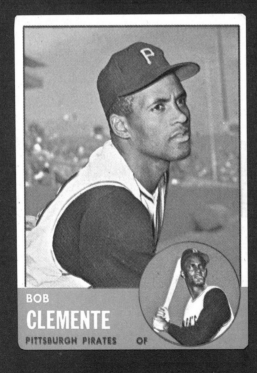

BOB
CLEMENTE
PITTSBURGH PIRATES   OF

Carroll Hardy holds the singular distinction of being the only man ever to pinch hit for Ted Williams, which on the face of it might seem ridiculous unless you stop to consider that Williams was injured at the time and that the Red Sox didn't have anybody better they could put up to bat. No, on second thought I take it all back. It **is** ridiculous.

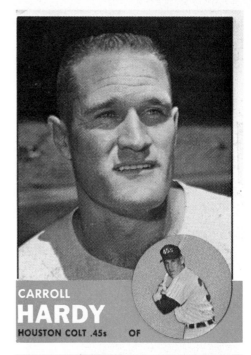

CARROLL
HARDY
HOUSTON COLT .45s   OF

Clint Courtney had not one, but two nicknames — "Scrap Iron" and the "Toy Bulldog" — both of which, curiously enough, fit perfectly. He was a feisty, combative little catcher with the Browns and Senators during the mid-fifties who tried to make up for his playing deficiencies with generous doses of what the hard rock disciplinarians in the athletic realm like to refer to as "leadership qualities."

In other words, he was noisy.

Every high school team has a guy like this — usually a short, muscular, pimpled, second-string catcher whose specialty it is to assure you when your team is behind 23-2 that "this thing isn't over yet" or "we're starting to get to this guy now," and who delight in short, pithy exhortations like "how to chuck 'em" and "way to fire" and "let's hear a little chatter out there, kid." They are also given to intense displays of unwarranted physical activity, from excessive fanny-patting to threats to lay someone out in the dugout. Fortunately these little bastions of insecurity are usually prevented by their lack of talent from progressing much further than the sandlots, although occasionally one will leak into organized ball. They make terrific fans when their playing days are over though, almost as if this had been their true calling all along. They always come to the game with a transistor radio, drink a lot of beer, heckle loudly, and somehow or other inevitably manage to end up sitting right behind me.

CLINT *Courtney*
WASHINGTON SENATORS   C.

In 1960 Mike Fornieles was one of the premier relief pitchers in the American League—fireman of the year, 10-5 record, 14 saves, 70 appearances, 2.64 earned run average, voted overwhelmingly to the American League All Star team.

The next year he hurt his arm and his earned run average almost doubled.

In 1963 he went to spring training with the Red Sox, tried to throw hard, couldn't, was sent down to the minors, hit hard, and released.

Two months later I watched him pitch for the Supreme Diner Saints, a Boston semi-pro pickup team whose maximum salary was $25 a night.

The moral of the story is

(1) it's a tough life

(2) save your money

(3) and, as my old friend Angelo Cartolucci used to tell me, when reflecting on the gyrating intricacies of the New York stock and bond markets—kid, in this business you got to wear your tennis shoes.

Whenever my father would take us up to Canada during summer vacations, we would always pass through a small sleepy potato-farming town in northern Maine near the Canadian border called Cherryfield—the sort of place that was inhabited exclusively by lobster fishermen and grizzly bears. Over the main street of the town—which coincidentally was the only street in the town—there was a huge white muslin banner strung between the Flying A Gas Station sign and the front of the McKeither Brothers Dry Goods Store that proclaimed in faded red script: WELCOME TO CHERRYFIELD, MAINE, HOME OF MAJOR LEAGUE PITCHER CARLTON WILLEY. For this reason, and for none other that I can possibly think of, I have always been a fan of Carlton Willey's. And even though, in the manner of all my particular and special sporting favorites, he has always managed somehow to disappoint me, I cannot help thinking that nothing he could do, no matter how dismal or mediocre, could ever prove disappointing, in any way, shape or form, to the people of Cherryfield, Maine.

Frank Baumann was a charter member of the "He Lost It in the Army" club—a curious assortment of mediocre ballplayers that resurrects itself every ten years or so, shortly after the United States has managed to extricate itself once again, more or less successfully, from another round of debilitating foreign entanglements. Membership in the club is open to any ballplayer who has ever belonged to any armed service for any length of time and who now plays lousy. The player in question is entitled by his membership to be excused by press, radio, television, management, and himself for his inept performances with the explanation that, although he was a red hot prospect at the time of his entry into his country's service, somehow the time spent away from the game and the tremendous burden of his military duties have dulled his almost superhuman physical prowess. Members are never established players—who seem curiously immune to the sapping effects of these prolonged layoffs—but always untried youngsters—bonus babies and highly touted rookies—whom owners and general managers have been promoting ruthlessly in an effort to prop up the rapidly diminishing reputations of their sagging franchises. Frank Baumann was a member in good standing of the Korean War chapter of the club—stateside division, one oak-leaf cluster. The story on him was that he had lost the velocity on his fast ball while sitting around some of Mother Army's more decrepit southern encampments on his ample derriere while other less talented and less patriotic youngsters were gaining good seasoning experience in the low minors. (Actually I have always thought that a more cogent explanation for his arm problems might have been that he injured it by lifting a particularly hefty forkful of mashed potatoes up to his bovine craw.)

Harry "Peanuts" Lowrey might have been a grain salesman if he hadn't gone into organized baseball. He played for thirteen years with a number of teams, and is best remembered, if remembered at all, for his pinch hitting. In 1952 and 1953 Peanuts led the league in pinch hits. The nickname had to do with the fact that most all of those pinch hits were singles, but I'm sure his managers were happy to take them any way they came.

Dick Farrell, "Turk," from Boston, was a fireballer in the truest sense of the term. I would not have gone to the plate when he pitched. Turk had 1,137 strike-outs over the course of his thirteen year career, many of them directly attributable to naked fear on the part of the opposing batters. He had a fast ball that involved all of his energy and strength, and it is remarkable that even in his final years as a reliever with Houston, and finally with the Phillies again, Turk could still cause his catchers to put a piece of sponge in their mitts so as to better withstand the sting of his ball.

DICK FARRELL
Pitcher

Los Angeles
Dodgers

"Sport" magazine once commissioned Gussie Moran to do a piece on the ten handsomest players in major league baseball. Now, you may think that this has nothing to do with sport—and in a way you'd be right—but then again you never had to go to press once a month either, and can you imagine how sick the editors down at "Sport" must have gotten of articles like: "Bob Richards, the Vaulting Parson," and "Walter Alston Wonders—Is Andy Pafko Really over the Hill?" I mean, I know how sick **I** got of them, and I only had to read them. Anyway it is my recollection that Bobby Avila was Miss Moran's choice as the player she'd most like to be caught in a rundown with (something about finely chiseled olive features and darkly brooding Inca eyes) although I know for sure that Jimmy Piersall, Bob Friend, and Jerry Coleman were in there somewhere too, perhaps sandwiched in between Bobo Newsom and Tito Francona in the baby-face domestic division. I was sort of miffed that she had made no mention of Don Mossi. Bobby Avila was a very good second baseman for the Cleveland Indians for about ten years before he was traded to the Boston Red Sox where he promptly proceeded to become an old man in about three weeks.

Bob Purkey had to do a lot to live down his name. Over 13 seasons with the Pirates, the Reds, and the Cardinals he put together a won-lost record of 129–115, and his best year came in 1962, when he was 23–5, with a 2.81 ERA. Bob finished his career with the team he began it with, Pittsburgh, his home town. I have a weakness, as you might have noticed, for baseball stories involving home-town players making good. That was a fantasy that I developed as I practiced my pitching against a brick wall in my eleventh year.

BOB PURKEY pitcher

AL ZARILLA

Al Zarilla is the only player in the history of the American League to hit two triples in one inning. He is also the only player in the history of the American League to be traded from one team to another on two separate occasions—from the Athletics to the Red Sox—once in 1949 and once again in 1952. These are as obscure a pair of records as you are likely to come up with, and you may make of them what you wish.

Jim Bouton is a big mouth.

When I was born, Sherm Lollar was catching for the White Sox. When I first went off to grammar school, Sherm Lollar was catching for the White Sox. When I was confirmed, Sherm Lollar was catching for the White Sox. And when I graduated from high school, Sherm Lollar was still catching for the White Sox. At some point during my adolescence it suddenly crossed my mind that Sherm Lollar had probably always caught for the White Sox, that in fact there had always been a White Sox and Sherm Lollar had always been their catcher. It also began occurring to me at around this same time that when, in the not too distant future, my time of terminal reckoning had finally arrived, and I lay wrinkled and wheezing on my fingertip adjustable death bed, Sherm Lollar was six-to-five to come walking into the room, resplendent in burnt orange knee pads and chest protector, smile his slow, patient, elderly uncle smile through the gnarled bands of his catcher's mask and tag me out for the final time with a grass-stained Spaulding American League baseball.

Imagine my surprise to learn that Sherm Lollar is no longer catching for the White Sox. That he has been replaced by platoons of anonymous visaged imposters with strange-sounding names like Camilo Carreon, J. C. Martin, Johnny Romano, and Jerry McNertney. Well, it just goes to show you that nothing really lasts anymore.

Once, just once, I would like to have heard Eddie Lebaron's name mentioned by Lindsey Nelson or Mel Allen or George Ratterman without

HARRY SIMPSON

outfield **KANSAS CITY A'S**

DICK HALL

KANSAS CITY ATHLETICS   PITCHER

DAVE PHILLEY

outfield **BALTIMORE ORIOLES**

their preceding it with the standard obligatory diminuendo.

Little Eddie Lebaron. Tiny Eddie Lebaron. Pint-sized Eddie Lebaron.

For fifteen years I thought Little was Eddie Lebaron's first name.

And once, just once, as long as we're dealing in pointless adolescent fantasies, I would like to see a baseball card of Harry Simpson which does not have a picture on the back of Harry carrying a suitcase.

Suitcase Simpson.

"How'd you happen to get that nickname anyway, Harry?"

"Gee, Mel, I haven't got the slightest idea."

I know, I know.

It's too much for anyone to expect.

The William and McGeorge Bundy Memorial Tweed Salami for Creative Cloudy Thinking goes again this year to Dick Hall, the 6'6" itinerant relief pitcher and Swarthmore graduate who, when asked by Pirate manager Fred Haney why he had ignored three separate and distinct steal signals flashed to him during the preceding inning, replied: "I didn't think you meant it."

Dave Philley played for eighteen years in the majors, most of them in the American League, and two that I remember in particular with the Philadelphia Athletics, the second of which saw him hit .303 as the regular left fielder. He was traded away, only to return to Philadelphia in 1958, to play for the Phillies, and that's when those fans who remember him first thought of him as Philley of the Phillies, of course.

Bill Skowron was, unless you count Norm Siebern (which I don't think anybody does), the last really good Yankee first baseman. Before him came Lou Gehrig, Hal Chase, and Johnny Mize. After him came Buddy Barker, Joe Pepitone, and Harry Bright. So you can see the quality does tend to fall off here quite a bit.

Skowron was called Moose because he looked like . . . well, a moose. He was the only one of the many modern-day athletes who have had this nickname incidentally who actually deserved it. He was also the only man I have ever seen who had muscles in his nose. Bill Skowron was in fact musclebound. This curious malady, which most of us have heard of without actually believing in, probably prevented him from achieving anything approaching his true potential. His iambix was forever interlocking with his metatarsis and throwing his digitalis out of whack. But it didn't stop him from turning in twelve solid years with the Yankees and one or two more with various and sundry National League teams.

Another thing about Skowron that has always stuck in my mind is that despite the fact that he played in New York he lived, for some reason or other, in New Jersey, a curious circumstance which seemed to my eleven-year-old way of looking at things (and guided by my highly underdeveloped sense of geography) the very height of urban athletic sophistication.

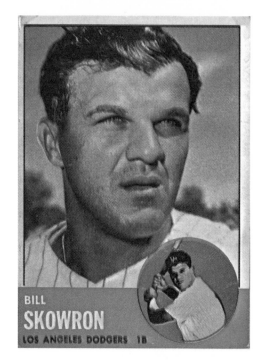

BILL
SKOWRON
LOS ANGELES DODGERS 1B

ED STANKY

Eddie Stanky defined spunk and persistence. The Brat got into more home-plate arguments with umpires than he hit home runs, but he did have his years, especially 1950 with the New York Giants, when he hit an even .300 and led the league in walks. He stood close to the plate, daring pitchers to brush him back or hit him, and if they did either, he was out to the mound, bat in hand, to discuss pitching with them. He managed major league teams twice, and those years were characterized by the same fire and excitement as his playing years. Eddie Stanky was one of baseball's most colorful players and his spirit enlivened its leisurely pace.

Rocky Bridges looked like a ballplayer. In fact he probably looked more like a ballplayer than any ballplayer who ever lived. His head looked like a sack full of rusty nails, he kept about six inches of chewing tobacco lodged permanently in the upper recesses of his left cheek, and his uniform always looked as if he had just slept in it—which of course he probably had. He had a squat muscular frame, a wire-brush crew cut, and a glower that could have intimidated Ty Cobb. He was the sort of guy who would spike his own grandmother to break up a double play. Whenever I saw him kneeling eagerly in the on-deck circle, his knobby little hands kneading the handle of his Louisville Slugger, his baggy pants hiked up almost to the midpoint of his barrel-like chest, his baseball cap cocked slightly askew and tipped to a notably unraffish angle, it would occur to me that in reality Rocky Bridges did not exist, that he was in fact a character from a Ring Lardner short story, or a punch line to a Grantland Rice anecdote, or a figment of Damon Runyon's imagination. Some glorious throwback to a more basic and less stylized era. I understand that Rocky is now managing with some degree of success in the lower minors, and I for one would like to wish him all the luck that is so obviously his due. I suppose, however, that it is only a matter of time now before I open up my sports pages some sad Monday morning and am greeted, over my Maltex and raisin toast, by a picture of Rocky resplendent in sideburns, moustache, and purple velour jumpsuit posing for publicity stills in Paducah, Kentucky, or West Laramee, Wyoming, with some heavy-thighed, bouffant-tressed ball girl. But oh please, dear God, please, just don't let him be carrying a shoulder bag.

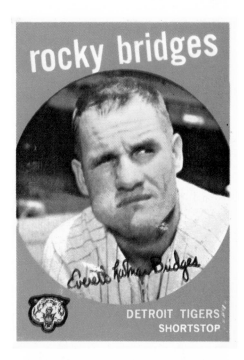

In the seventy-five or so years that the World Series has been in existence there have been perhaps 1,200 pitchers who have pitched in it. Of these, Don Larsen is the only one to have pitched a perfect game. Like Sophia Loren's marriage to Carlo Ponti, the continuing popularity of Danny Thomas, and the political career of Spiro Agnew, there is no rational explanation for this. It just is.

DALE MITCHELL

outfield **CLEVELAND INDIANS**

Dale Mitchell

Dale Mitchell was the man whom Don Larsen struck out to end his perfect game. The newsreel film of this event, which I have seen perhaps fifty times or so over the past fifteen years, shows Larsen stretching wearily into his newly developed no-wind-up delivery, letting fly with a medium-speed sinker, catching the outside corner of the plate, and then rushing jubilantly off the mound and into the waiting arms of a wildly leaping Yogi Berra. Mitchell—a line drive hitting outfielder and pinch hitter with a number of major league ball clubs over the course of a lengthy if unmemorable career, and the last man, by reason of his reputation for always getting a piece of the ball, you would expect to take a call third strike under these particular circumstances—can be seen at the bottom of the frame, bending forward slightly into the break of the pitch, holding back at the last second with his swing and then staring back incredulously at the umpire as if refusing to believe that a pitcher with Don Larsen's stuff could possibly strike him out under any circumstances. The camera then pans up over the raucous celebrations in the Yankee infield and Dale Mitchell, the image and the reality, disappears permanently from the scope of the camera, as well as from the minds, hearts, and feelings of an ungrateful and short-memoried American public.

"SANDY" KOUFAX *pitcher* **BROOKLYN DODGERS**

This is Sandy Koufax's Bar Mitzvah picture. The uniform was a present from his grandmother.

Everybody knows that pitchers aren't supposed to hit. There are some exceptions to the rule, of course — Babe Ruth, Ted Williams, and Stan Musial, converted pitchers all, were among the greatest hitters the game has ever known. But then again, they were **converted** pitchers. Of course, there are some pitchers who remain pitchers who can hit — Warren Spahn, Bob Lemon, and Don Newcombe come most readily to mind — while still retaining their ability to get opposing batters out. But they are a commodity in particularly short supply and well worth their weight in Ernie Oravetz fungo bats. Then there are those pitchers who can hit like a whiz but aren't too good at the pitching end of things — Jerry Casale, Maury McDermott, Bob Chakales. This is known as reversing your priorities and can only end in disappointment for the practitioner. But saddest of all and most numerous by far are the pitchers who can neither pitch nor hit. Hank Aguirre achieved some modest success in the late fifties and early sixties with the Detroit Tigers. He had a moderate fast ball, fair breaking stuff, and pretty good control, and as long as he managed to maintain the delicate balance among these less than overwhelming gifts he could survive in the big leagues. But the boy could not hit. I mean to tell you, he couldn't even get close. He once struck out something like fifteen straight times and received a standing ovation for hitting a foul ball. They kept his statistics by computing not the number of hits he got but the number of times he made contact with the ball.

Some of my other favorite lousy hitting pitchers of the fifties were John Tsitouris, Dean Stone, and Johnny Klippstein. This, of course, is not even to mention Dean Chance, who came to bat 75 times in 1965 and struck out 56 of them, or Ron Herbel, who in his six years in major league baseball up until 1968 had been to bat 165 times with 5 hits and 102 strike-outs. This gave him a lifetime batting average of .030 and a lifetime strike-out average of .617.

Way to go, Ron.

Pssst! Neil Chrisley's real first name was Barbra.
Pass it on.

HANK Aguirre
CLEVELAND INDIANS PITCHER

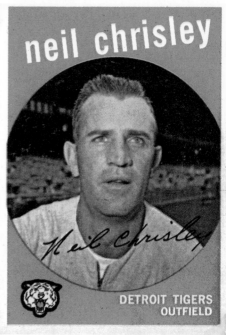

neil chrisley

DETROIT TIGERS
OUTFIELD

In 1959 some sad-souled individuals of my acquaintance who have the calamitous and double-pronged ill fortune of living in Bay Shore, Long Island, New York, while being at the same time inveterate Yankee fans, had a fairly good-sized pool going among themselves, the object of which was to determine the precise number of games it would require for Hector Lopez, the suicidally inept Yankee third baseman, to seriously maim, cripple, or otherwise disfigure himself while patrolling the hot corner at Yankee Stadium.

Now, it is not necessary for me to declare that Hector Lopez was the worst fielding third baseman in the history of baseball. Everyone knows that. It is more or less a matter of public record. But I do feel called upon somehow to try and indicate, if only for the historical archivists among us, the sheer depths of his innovative barbarousness. Hector Lopez was quite literally a butcher. Pure and simple. A butcher. His range was about one step to either side, his hands seemed to be made of concrete, and his defensive attitude was so cavalier and so arbitrary as to hardly constitute an attitude at all. Hector did not simply field a ground ball, he attacked it. Like a farmer trying to kill a snake with a stick. And his mishandling of routine infield flies was the sort of thing of which legends are made. Hector Lopez was not just a bad fielder for a third baseman. In fact, Hector Lopez was not just a bad fielder for a baseball player. Hector Lopez was, when every factor has been taken into consideration, a bad fielder for a human being. The stands are full of obnoxious leather-lunged cretins who insist they can play better than most major leaguers. Well, in Hector's case they could have been right. I would like to go on record right here and now as declaring Hector Lopez the all-time worst fielding major league ballplayer.

That's quite a responsibility there, Hector, but I have every confidence you'll be able to live up to it.

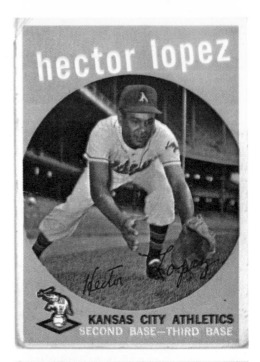

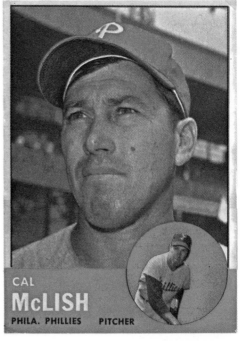

"The Golden Glow of Wretched Excess," or "Some Baby Names We Wish Had Never Been Thought Of." Cal McLish's full name was Calvin Coolidge Julius Caesar Tuskahoma McLish.

If you can pick out a thread running through all that, then you are definitely a better man than I.

Jesus McFarlane was a living testimonial, on the other hand, to the fact that naming your child after a famous celebrity does not necessarily help.

Gene Stephens was the ultimate caddy, or scrub — which is the baseball equivalent of the fag (if you'll pardon the expression), or new boy, in the English public school system. It is the caddy's sole function in life to come in as a substitute in the late innings of a hopelessly lopsided game, to act as a defensive replacement for an aging power hitter, or to pinch run for a slow-witted second-string catcher with varicose veins. For accomplishing these varied and undemanding assignments with a minimum of carping and a maximum of efficiency, the caddy is permitted by management to sit at the back of the team bus, to have his uniform cleaned by the assistant to the assistant equipment manager, and to dream on unencumbered of one day working his way into the starting lineup himself. Caddys are generally fleet-footed, weak-hitting outfielders whose ambitions far outstrip their abilities. Being human, they desire to be stars. And, being human, they are never quite realistic enough to realize the hopelessness of their situation. Some notable caddies of the preceding era were: Jim Pyburn, Al Pilarcik, and Sam Bowens with Baltimore; Chuck Essegian, Al Luplow, and Don Dillard with Cleveland; Fred Valentine, Bud Zipfel, and Dan Dobbek with Washington; and Joe Nossek, Chuck Diering, and Gary Geiger with just about everybody. Gene Stephens held Ted Williams' glove for seven long humiliating seasons during the Splinter's splendid decline. This is indeed a long term of servitude, even for a caddy. He finally got his big shot at the limelight in 1960 when he was traded to the Baltimore Orioles and proceeded, in the manner of all caddies, to blow it. (Play me or trade me.) During the late fifties the Red Sox had two other full-time caddies of note — Marty Keough for Jim Piersall, and Faye Throneberry for Jackie Jensen. It was Throneberry's extra burden in life to be the brother, in spirit as well as in flesh, to Marvelous Marv Throneberry, the non plus ultra of New York Met first basemen.

Fabulous Faye!

107

FRED HATFIELD

second base DETROIT TIGERS

Fred Hatfield was a slightly less than mediocre second baseman with the Red Sox and the Tigers in the mid-fifties. His idea of good clean fun was to taunt Jim Piersall with endless streams of nuthouse motif humor from the relative safety of the Detroit dugout. This is the type of behavior one can expect of a man with a .242 lifetime batting average who wears the number 1 on his uniform. It takes all kinds, as I am constantly reminding myself. And this, in more ways than one, is something of a shame.

Walt Dropo, big Moose from Moosup, Connecticut, was one of my special favorites, although I never saw him play. Actually, the only time I ever thought of him was when I opened a pack of cards and saw that I had gotten another card of him, probably my twentieth, and couldn't trade any of them to any of my friends because they too already had nineteen more than they needed. Moose, in the Kluszewski tradition, was a first baseman, put there where he wouldn't be called upon to move around much, because in Moose's case, at 6′5″ and 220 pounds (which was his weight as a rookie, I'm sure, or maybe back in the early days of his youth at Moosup), it wasn't all that easy to move around.

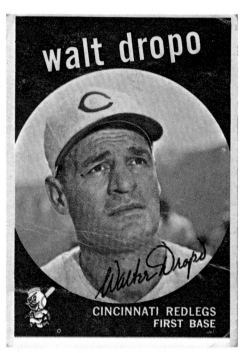

walt dropo

CINCINNATI REDLEGS
FIRST BASE

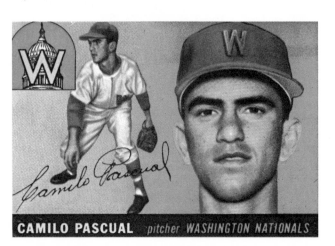

CAMILO PASCUAL *pitcher* WASHINGTON NATIONALS

Hey Mac, you wanna buy a hot Buick?

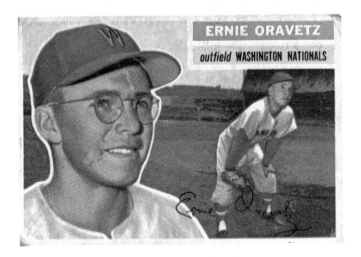

ERNIE ORAVETZ

outfield WASHINGTON NATIONALS

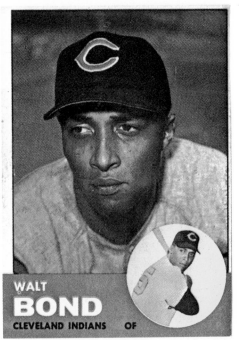

WALT
BOND
CLEVELAND INDIANS   OF

The short and the tall of it.

Walt Bond was a 6'7", 230-pound outfielder–first baseman who spent six years in the majors trying to prove that bad things can come in big packages too. As you can probably tell by this picture, he wasn't all that crazy about chewing tobacco either.

Ernie Oravetz on the other hand carried petiteness to an illogical extreme. He was a 5'4" 145-pound outfielder who was built like Cubby O'Brien—only not as muscular. He played two years and 188 games in the Washington Senators lineup without ever hitting a home run. For those of you who might be wondering whatever became of little Ernie, I am happy to report that he is still very much connected with our national pastime. He works all the Dover (Delaware) Mud Hens' home games in an administrative capacity: popping out of the little hole behind home plate to hand the umpire a fresh supply of baseballs.

Tracy Stallard threw the pitch that Roger Maris hit for his sixty-first home run in 1961. This act and the resulting publicity that surrounded it saved Stallard's career from the profound and perpetual anonymity it so richly deserved. His final major league won-lost totals were 30 games won and 57 lost.

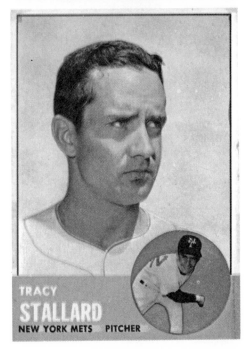

TRACY
STALLARD
NEW YORK METS   PITCHER

Smoky Burgess was fat. Not baseball fat like Mickey Lolich or Early Wynn. But FAT fat. Like the mailman or your Uncle Dwight. Putsy Fat. Slobby Fat. Just Plain Fat. In fact I would venture to say that Smoky Burgess was probably the fattest man ever to play professional baseball. Of course he was not always that fat; when he was a catcher with the Pittsburgh Pirates he was merely plump, the way a good hitting catcher can afford to be, you know, for blocking the plate and all that. But as Burgess grew older a curious tendency began to manifest itself in both his reflexes and his metabolism: as with most older players, of course, his coordination began to go, his arm grew weaker, his endurance lessened, his breathing shortened, his gut grew. But, unlike most aging players, his ability to hit the ball grew gradually greater. In fact, the older he got and the fatter he got, the better his hitting seemed to become, until at the age of thirty-eight Smoky weighed close to 300 pounds and was hitting over .320. Of course, a 300-pound man can hardly be expected—or allowed, for that matter—to play any rigorous sport full time. He is liable to hurt himself or, more likely, someone else. So Smoky Burgess became instead a full-time pinch hitter for the Chicago White Sox—and one of the best pinch hitters in all of baseball at that. The sight of him standing in the batter's box, his voluminous avoirdupois impinging on a full 45 percent of the natural strike zone, his stubby arms flailing out in that curiously hitched and compacted swing which made him look for all the world like a spastic rhinoceros beating a rug, and then tootling on down the first base line as another of his seeing-eye bleeders wends its way through a befuddled infield, is one that those who have been gifted to witness it are not likely to forget.

I don't have any idea what Smoky is doing these days (he retired finally in 1967), but I can tell you one thing for sure, he must certainly be an interesting and instructive sight, now that he's been out of baseball for a few years and has had a chance to get out of shape.

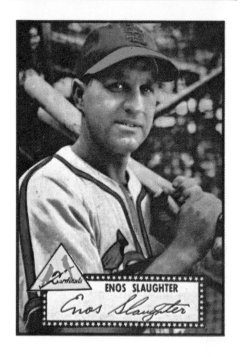

SMOKY BURGESS catcher

ENOS SLAUGHTER

Enos Slaughter's career spanned nineteen years, most of them spent with the Cardinals. He rarely missed a game as a right fielder, and had several seasons over .300. Enos was always good for extra-base hits, especially doubles, and always when the team needed them. He was a good defensive player, with no concern for the hardness of outfield walls in his pursuit of long fly balls.

I remember my mother telling me once that she knew she was getting old when all the policemen started looking young. Well, lately I have begun to notice that all the first- and third-base coaches in the major leagues have a decidedly youngish tinge about them —much more so than those somber-visaged, wrinkly pantsed father figures of my youth. I mean, whatever happened to Don Gutteridge, Luman Harris, and Frankie Crosetti anyway? And what's this I hear about Gus Bell's son Buddy playing the outfield for the Cleveland Indians? What nonsense! Gus Bell's too young to have a son, for God's sake. Hey, have any of you guys seen Wally Post lately?

Then there is the case of Rich Rollins, who, it seems to me, was a rookie third baseman with the Minnesota Twins about fifteen minutes ago. Well here I am still sitting around like a fool waiting for him to reach his full potential and it turns out he's been retired and coaching for the past several seasons. I thought he was just out of the lineup with the chicken pox or something, and all this time he's been turning into a senior citizen behind my back. So anyway, what I really want to know is, if Rich Rollins is now an old man, does that mean it's too late for me?

Unlike most players of undistinguished habit, Dale Long was granted two separate and distinct moments of baseball glory. The first came when he hit home runs in eight consecutive ball games for the Pirates in 1956, thus establishing a new major league record. The second came when he was picked up late in his career (1962) by the New York Yankees for their annual late September pennant drive and proceeded to propel them almost singlehandedly into the World Series against the Dodgers. He now hosts a nightly ten-minute sports roundup for an Albany, New York, television station, reading long lists of A.P. box scores, Saratoga High School track team results, and Scolharie County fishing reports in the same flat, colorless style that always characterized his play around the first base bag.

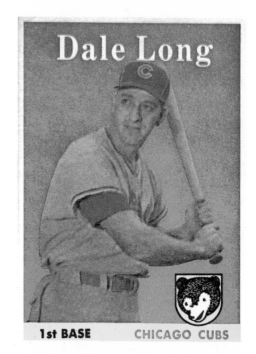

1st BASE   CHICAGO CUBS

There is a saying around the racetrack—horses for courses—which translates roughly: every dog has his day, given the proper environment. The horse (or dog) in question here is Felix Mantilla, a tall, spindly legged Puerto Rican infielder with limited range and an even more limited throwing arm, who after eight lackluster years in the National League (29 career home runs, .245 lifetime batting average), spent most of the 1964 and 1965 seasons lofting lazy fly balls up, off and over the friendly left-field wall at Fenway Park. If ever there was a swing that was tailor-made for a ball park, it was Felix's that was made for Fenway. Of course, eventually the opposing pitchers started spotting him low and away on the outside part of the plate, and Felix's green monster swing began to lose some of its highly artificial luster, but before it had gone sour completely the deleterious Boston flesh peddlers who had secured his services during a mid-winter trade with the Mets for three snow tires and a bottle of Roquefort dressing had managed to unload him at the top like an over-inflated growth stock on the latest expansionist patsies—the Houston Colt 45s. Somehow or other Felix never quite got the hang of the Astrodome.

FELIX
MANTILLA
BOSTON RED SOX   INF-OF

112

It is the fate of men such as Tommie Aaron, Hank Allen, and Vince DiMaggio, men who—if I may be permitted to put it in its frankest, most unflattering light—have seen fit to carry sibling rivalry far beyond the bonds of ordinary common sense, always to be referred to by their full names—as in TOMMIE Aaron or HANK Allen, with the emphasis on the TOMMIE and the HANK—while their teammates and older brothers are allowed to luxuriate in the relative stability of their surnames alone. Aaron, Allen, DiMaggio. Dennis Hull is always going to be DENNIS Hull just as Earl Averill, Jr., is always going to be Earl Averill, JR. It goes with the territory. Of course it wasn't bad enough that Tommie Aaron should have chosen to follow in the illustrious footsteps of his brother Henry, who is at this very moment closing in inexorably on Babe Ruth's 714 career home-run record, but that he should have chosen to do so on the same team as his brother, at the same time, and in the same position can only be described as a needless and willful public self-humiliation.

Tommy, why?

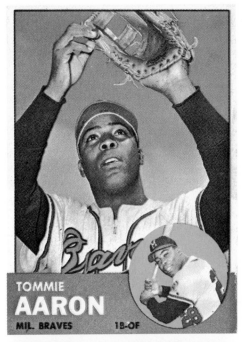

Robin Roberts is now the baseball coach at my old high school in a suburb of Philadelphia, and that, in addition to causing my thoughts to stray toward the short span of time we have allotted to us for living on this earth, is somehow appropriate. The main summer baseball idol of my youth, Robin Roberts was the best pitcher in the National League in the first half of the fifties. A 20-game winner for six consecutive seasons with the Phillies, beginning with the pennant year, the Whiz Kids' 1950, Robin Roberts was class, and when his turn in the rotation came up, you'd be lucky to get a ticket to Philadelphia's Shibe Park, even to see last-place Pittsburgh.

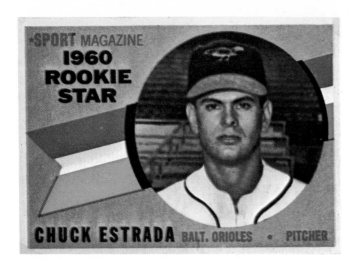

The life of the hard-throwing, young, breaking-ball pitcher in the major leagues is often nasty, brutish, and short. I offer the names of Bob Grim, Dick Drott, Tom Sturdivant, and Dave "Boo" Ferriss as testimony to this depressing supposition. For a while during the late fifties and early sixties the Baltimore Orioles seemed to have a monopoly on promising young pitchers who developed arm trouble—Wally Bunker, Steve Barber, Tom Phoebus, and Jim Hardin, to name just a few. Even Dave McNally and Jim Palmer flirted for a time with tendonitis and torn ligaments—Palmer falling as low as the Florida Instructional League in 1968 in an attempt, rarely successful, to restore his damaged limb. But probably the hardest loss of all for the Orioles to take was that of Chuck Estrada. Estrada was 18–11 and 15–9 in '60 and '61 respectively before developing a sore elbow in 1963 at the tender age of twenty-five. Any pitching coach will tell you that, while shoulder trouble is pretty bad and upper arm trouble is even worse, when the demon elbow begins its mordant mournful throb, it's good night, Irene. Estrada tried two comebacks in '66 and '67 with the Cubs and the Mets. His records were 1–1 and 1–2 respectively, with earned run averages of 7.30 and 9.41.

Good night, Chuck.

Cal Abrams was the Jewish Gino Cimoli.

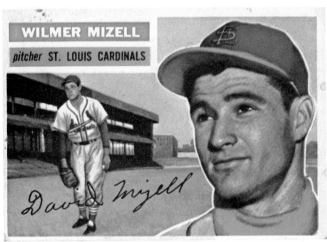

Gino Cimoli was the Italian Ossie Chavarria.

There is an old and treasured custom among the participants of both major leagues of nicknaming a player after his place of birth. Fortunately this custom is confined to folksy, slow-talking players of southern origin or else we would be faced with a continuing flow of stories in the "Sporting News" dealing with the minor triumphs and tragedies of Gene "Santa Barbara" Lillard or Vic "West Springfield" Raschi. All of this, of course, in no way explains why Wilmer Mizell was nicknamed "Vinegar Bend" since his hometown was Leakesville, Mississippi. On the other hand, maybe it does. To confuse matters even more, Mr. Mizell, or "Vinegar Bend," or Wilmer, has seen fit to sign his autograph on this card as David Mizell. Well, whatever you wish to call him he was a pleasing and individualistic performer and a man of great wit and geniality. Such geniality, in fact, that in 1962 after a so-so National League career consisting of 90 wins and 88 losses, 680 walks and 918 strikeouts, he took himself, his sly grin and his weary left arm out of professional baseball altogether and into the halls of the United States Congress where sly ginning, slow-talking southerners with country nicknames and folksy mannerisms are much more appreciated than they are just about anywhere else. Now every year he pitches the House Republicans to victory over their Democratic colleagues in the annual congressional baseball game. How 'bout that, Dickie "San Clemente" Nixon?

Harvey Kuenn was a professional hitter, a professional hitter, by definition, being any man who can calculate his batting average to the third decimal point on his way down to first base after a single. Harvey Kuenn had 2,052 hits in his major league career, all but three of which were singles. These three should have been singles also, but the outfielders who ran in to pick them up misplayed them into doubles. The singles hitter is the lost soul of professional baseball, the leper of the live ball era. In golf you drive for show and putt for dough. In baseball you pop for show and plough for dough. This depressing and inequitable happenstance enables boorish muscular clowns with overinflated reputations and 90° angle swings like Dick Stuart and Joe Pepitone to drive Cadillacs and eat caviar while solid if unspectacular practitioners of the round-ball arts like Bob Boyd and Heeney Majeski are walking and eating Wheatena.

My favorite banjo hitters of the fifties were Pete Runnels, who batted over .300 six years in a row without ever hitting a ball more than 150 feet; Don Mueller, who once got a base hit on an intentional walk; and Bob Dillinger, who, despite the fact that he had a lifetime .306 batting average, nobody—except his mother and me—seems to remember at all.

Jack Meyer is, for me, one of those bittersweet baseball memories, like Herb Score. He was the local boy who'd made it when he was called up from a Phillies' farm club and came back to his home town to pitch for the home team. And certainly his first season was exciting: he was responsible for saving 16 games as a reliever. But the six years that followed showed no improvement, even though he had good stuff and everybody was for him. The final act came when he was killed in an automobile accident in 1967, appropriately enough, in Philadelphia.

Some ballplayers exist in my memory not so much for the wonder of their accomplishments on the playing field as for the peculiar tenuity of their baseball cards. Ferris Fain, for example, was a ping-hitting first baseman for a number of teams in the American League during the fifties who, through a mysterious set of contrary circumstances, managed somehow to win the American League batting championship in consecutive years 1951 and 1952, with averages of .344 and .327, even though he had never hit over .291 in any full major league season before or since. This, plus the fact that he had been an amateur boxer in his younger days in Walnut Creek, California and was nicknamed — rather cruelly I always thought, but nonetheless justifiably — "Burrhead," was all I knew, or quite frankly cared to know, about Ferris Fain. It was his somber and blurred representation on this 3 × 5 piece of wilted cardboard laminate that aroused my adolescent enthusiasm far in excess of his own dreary, pedestrian reality. The year after he won the batting championship for the first time — 1952 — Ferris Fain was absolutely impossible to get in the greater Boston area. I don't know whether this was because the bubble-gum people had planned it this way or because of some mysterious distribution difficulties or whether it was just due to a general run of bad luck, but I do know that it was well into August and roughly $8.60 worth of bubble-gum purchases before I finally got my hands on a single Ferris Fain (thus achieving the enviable distinction incidentally of being the only kid in my neighborhood to own both a 1952 Ferris Fain and a 1951 Vern Bickford).

This card happened to be one of the last things that my brother held in his hands before his sore throat and swollen glands were diagnosed as the mumps several days later. For this reason it had to be burned. I don't think I want to talk about it anymore.

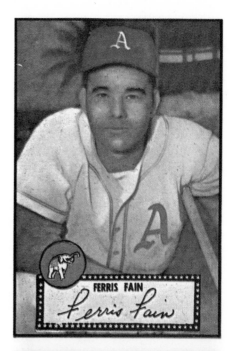

Solly Hemus was the poor man's Eddie Stanky — a good fielding, steady-hitting infielder with the Cardinals and the Phillies in the fifties. He had a temper as short as Stanky's and as much of an inclination to fight. Watching him chattering encouragement to his pitcher from his position at short, you knew that he'd be a manager someday, and he was, for the 1959–1961 Cardinals.

Remember when some guy you knew would tell you that a girl he was trying to fix you up with had a nice personality? That was the kiss of death, right?

Well, it was a lot like that with baseball cards too. Sometimes you had to read a little between the lines to get an accurate feel for what was really going on.

Take for example Sam Esposito—a diminutive, inept, but rather lovable little utility infielder with the White Sox from 1952 to 1963. In ten full major league seasons Sam got to bat a grand total of 792 times, for an average of 79.2 times per year, or once every 2 ballgames. He had a .207 lifetime batting average, 8 career homers, and a slugging average of .277, which—to put it mildly—is quite a bit short of spectacular. And what does Topps have to say about the awesome purveyor of these prestigious statistics? Well, here is a brief selection of their biographical comments with a translation into meaningful English.

"Sam joined the White Sox in 1952 and then was farmed out for the next two seasons before returning to Chicago."

Not a good beginning. Definitely downbeat and patronizing. Notice the distinct lack of enthusiasm for his major league prospects and the total disregard of his minor league record. The use of the term "farmed out" is an unhealthy sign also, connoting as it does a certain patina of failure. This is an expression which is rarely used and a situation which is rarely touched upon in baseball cards.

"He has proven to be a valuable hand, starting his share of games at as many as four positions."

This is known as damning with faint praise. The key terms here are "valuable hand," which can be translated roughly as bum, and "his share," which means very few. The mention of the four positions is also something of a sour note. Everybody knows that the composers of baseball card desiderata equate versatility with mediocrity.

"Sammy attended Indiana U. for three years."

Death. When they start mentioning a player's educational background we know we're dealing with a real stiff. After all, nobody cares whether or not Stan Musial ever got out of the second grade or that Dizzy Dean had a degree in quantum mechanics from Cambridge. They're just trying to divert our attention.

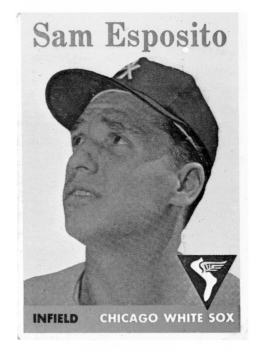

INFIELD   CHICAGO WHITE SOX

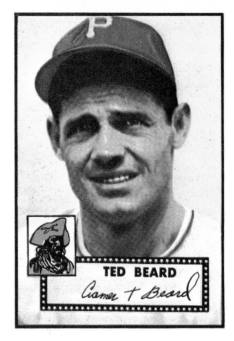

TED BEARD

But as long as they were at it, did they have to throw in the "three years"? This makes it sound as if Sammy was expelled.

"It's tough to bunt when he's playing third."

Yeah, and it's tough to kill a grizzly bear with a water pistol.

And so on and on it goes, belaboring the painfully obvious, masking the damaging realities, inflating the occasional achievement, misinterpreting the total dismal record. Some of the finest examples of twentieth-century neo-realistic fiction are to be found on the back of 1950's baseball cards.

Ted Beard set no records during his 7-year career with the Pirates and the White Sox. In fact, his lifetime batting average was .198. But that is beside the point. Ted Beard was all that kept me from a complete set of Bowman baseball cards in 1951. His card and about fifteen others were issued late in the season, and in limited quantities, at least where I lived. I saw a Ted Beard once in the possession of a friend who was visiting me overnight, but there was no way I could "obtain" it from him. I never did get Ted Beard (and never invited my "friend" to spend the night again).

Ted Kluszewski, Big Klu, was one of the inevitable, perennial, big sluggers. At 6'2", 225 pounds, he wasn't graceful, and played the position so many musclebound sluggers have occupied—first base. So big were his biceps that, one horribly hot afternoon, Klu removed the short sleeves from his Cincinnati uniform and thereby caused the greatest public commotion since Clark Gable appeared in the movie "It Happened One Night" without an undershirt. He hit 49 home runs in 1954 and had 141 RBIs. He massively stalks the Reds' dugout even today, as an assistant to manager Sparky Anderson.

And a carton of chocolate Yoo-Hoo to the little round man whose feet almost touch the floor. Lawrence Peter Berra on his lack of an offensive philosophy: "There ain't nobody that can hit and think at the same time."

This is my favorite picture of Yogi. Paul Newman, eat your heart out.

TED KLUSZEWSKI
CINCINNATI REDLEGS 1st BASE

Yogi Berra

CATCHER NEW YORK YANKEES

By their swings you shall know them.

Every ballplayer, good, bad, or indifferent, reveals the underlying strengths and weaknesses of his personality by the way he stands in the batter's box. It was Eddie Yost's belief—one which I happen to share with him incidentally—that, everything taken into consideration, a fellow just can't be too careful nowadays. For this reason he absolutely refused to swing at any pitch outside the strike zone, or very many on the perimeter of the strike zone for that matter, and always, but always, led the American League in bases on balls. This finicky peculiarity made him an almost perfect lead-off man, a more or less flaccid and vacuous baseball personality, and a source of great and constant encouragement to me, whose lifelong campaign it has been to put more muscle into that deleterious dugout chestnut—"A walk is as good as a hit."

I once waited for an hour and fifteen minutes in the rain outside the Fenway Park visitors' exit just to get the Great Stroller's autograph. When he finally emerged from the Senators' clubhouse and I stuck my scorecard out in front of him to sign, he paused for a moment, looked down at my outstretched hands with a curiously suspicious expression, signed E. Yost next to a picture of Chuck Dressen, and strolled off with a rolling side-saddle lilt along the white asphalt dividing lines of the parking lot. I always had the feeling that if I had held that program just an inch or two lower he would have refused to touch the damn thing at all.

Jackie Jensen, on the other hand, was up there to take his cuts. Because of this he perennially led the Red Sox, and sometimes even the majors, in RBIs **and** double plays. The RBIs I could take. The double plays were another matter entirely.

Some other things that annoyed me about Jackie were his florid skin and pale kinky locks which made him look for all the world like a miniature Sonny Tufts, his inability to take any razzing at all from the cheap seats, which struck me as totally immature and unprofessional, his oversolicitous concern with his wife's well-being (he retired in 1960 just to be with her), and his well-publicized and self-admitted fear of flying, which seemed an indication of circumspection bordering on cowardice.

Now that I have had thirteen or fourteen years to grow up and reflect on a number of these attitudes, I find that my feelings about most of them have changed markedly, have in fact reversed themselves almost entirely. The things that I despised Jackie Jensen for in 1957 I now respect him for in 1973. Whether this is due to some new-found maturity on my part or is simply a result of the fact that I too have grown older and softer with the years, I do not know. I suspect it is a combination of the two.

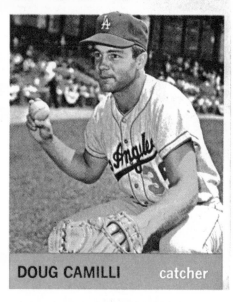

DODGERS

DOUG CAMILLI　　catcher

The most depressing of many depressing statistics in the annals of baseball's lengthy history belongs to one James Thomas Garry, a right-handed pitcher from Great Barrington, Massachusetts, who in his lone appearance in a major league uniform in 1893 pitched one inning for the Boston Nationals, gave up 5 hits, 4 walks, 7 runs, and took the loss. For this singularly iniquitous transgression Mr. Garry took with him to his cold and lonely grave a major league ERA of 63.00.

63.00!

The second most depressing statistic in the history of the sport belongs to Doug Camilli, the son of the great National League first baseman Dolf Camilli and certainly one of the weakest hitting catchers ever to don the tools of ignorance, in this era or any other. In eight major league seasons, five with Los Angeles Dodgers and three with the Washington Senators, the junior Camilli had a grand total of 18 home runs, 80 RBIs, and a corporate batting average of .199.

That's .199.

Not .200.

.199.

Think about that for a few minutes should you be trying to get yourself up for commiting suicide.

George Brunet was the Willy Loman of professional baseball. In a career which began in 1953 he played for twenty-three different minor and major league teams. Is it any wonder then that he always looked like the guy who had just missed the 12:15 to Massapequa?

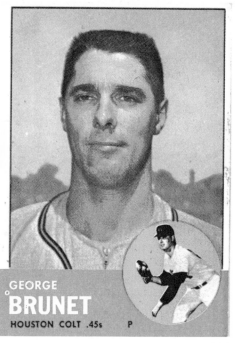

GEORGE BRUNET
HOUSTON COLT .45s　　P

Jim Gosger was a hustler. Not in the greater or Phil Spector sense, but in the lesser or Pete Rose sense. He was a painfully commonplace outfielder with the Red Sox and Athletics in the mid-sixties who never hit over .258 in the majors, averaged 6 home runs and 24 RBIs a year, had no power and no arm, bad reflexes and flat feet, was short and fat and slow, and looked exactly like the guy behind the cold-cut counter in your local Grand Union Supermarket. He was not a good hitter or a good baserunner or a good fielder. He was not even particularly skillful at calisthenics. In fact Jim Gosger did not possess any single outstanding athletic characteristic and by no stretch of the imagination did he ever at any time belong in the major leagues. The only problem was that nobody had ever bothered to tell Jim Gosger about this.

So he ran and he slid and he bunted and he hustled. He stretched singles into doubles and doubles into triples and moved runners along with opposite field grounders and almost killed himself diving for pop flies. He argued with umpires and heckled opposing pitchers and broke up double plays and let himself be hit by pitches. He stretched 29 cents worth of ability into a $15,000 annual salary, and a .175 minor league hitting stance into a respectable major league average. There are painfully few players like this. Most major league ballplayers, to the contrary, seem set upon systematically debilitating their talents. So it is refreshing, even inspiring on occasion, to come across an old-time hustler like Jim. It is depressing, however, to have to report that this year, at the not particularly advanced age of thirty, Jim Gosger has been passed over once again at the annual major league draft meetings in Honolulu, and that unless some sort of miracle occurs pretty soon he will be doing all his hustling from here on in at a decidedly lower level of competition.

Which brings me to a major point of contention.

If, as we have all so often been led to believe, it is not whether you win or lose but how you play the game, then how come the only way such outstanding practitioners of tireless and unselfish team play as Jim Gosger, Bob Elliott, and Danny O'Connell are ever going to get inside of Cooperstown is by paying their way in like all the rest of us.

Are them as has really the only ones as gets?

Billy Loes never would have gotten into the majors at all if they could have found someone to sign papers on him. He is to my knowledge the only ballplayer in the history of the National League ever to have lost a ground ball in the sun. What, if anything, do you think is going through his mind in this picture? Never mind, never mind. I don't want to know.

Pete Reiser made a career out of being injured. By far his favorite way of hurting himself was to run head-long into a concrete outfield fence at full speed in a futile attempt to catch a hopelessly uncatchable fly ball. Of course if an opportunity to employ this particular gambit was not immediately forthcoming, he could easily make do with sliding into third base and breaking his ankle. I have heard it said, in fact, concerning his masochistic proclivities, that on days when there was no game scheduled for Pete's particular team of the moment he would cheerfully pass the time in his hotel room by dropping large objects from great heights onto his toes. There is a little bit of this in most major league outfielders—Jim Piersall, Elmer Valo, and Ken Berry, to name a few recent examples — but in Reiser's case these overt self-destructive tendencies very nearly constituted a mania. The hard-core Brooklyn Dodger fans were great appreciators of this kind of frolicsome morbidity, however, and Pistol Pete was a great favorite in Flatbush.

Break Da Bum Up!

Curt Simmons, Robin Roberts' left-handed counter-part, was a mainstay of the Phillies' staff in the fifties. His high-kicking motion, quick-moving fast ball, and record six shutouts in 1952 all were clouded somewhat when, in an accident with a lawnmower in 1953, he cut off a toe. This threw his pitching balance off enough so that he never regained his form.

When Joe DiMaggio went off to the Army at the start of World War II, who do you think took his place?

Wrong.

It was Johnny Lindell.

And when Bill Dickey was called to his country's service in 1944, who would you guess succeeded him as the Yankee backstop?

Wrong again.

It was Mike Garbark.

And when Bob Feller was called away for his three years of military duty, what pitching immortal do you think Cleveland employed to plug his spot in the starting rotation?

No, I'm afraid you're going down for the third and final time.

It was Chubby Dean.

Well, Ted Williams, more patriotic and combative than the average run-of-the-mill ballplayer, managed to make it to the wars on two separate occasions, once for W.W.II and once again for Korea. His place in the Red Sox starting lineup was taken by, in 1942 Leon Culberson, and in 1952 Hoot Evers. Take it from me, folks, the way these two guys handled the situation you never would have known The Kid was gone.

"HOOT" EVERS
Walter 'Hoot' Evers

RUSS MEYER
pitcher CHICAGO CUBS

Russell Meyer

Russ Meyer was called "The Mad Monk" for reasons not totally clear to me. He was moderately successful as a pitcher for several National League teams in the fifties, and I remember in particular his very good fast ball for the Phillies during their glory year(s). Russ had a knack for signing on with pennant winners: the Phillies in 1950 and the Brooklyn Dodgers in 1953 and 1955. He also had a knack for getting injured (ankle, shoulder, back) and one felt that he was one of those players who might have been a star if only . . .

This is one of my all-time favorite cards. How do you suppose they got those baseballs to stay up there anyway? Nails? Scotch tape? Postage stamp hinges?

And why do you think Gus is giving us the high sign? Is he trying to assure us that everything is OK? Is he trying to indicate to us that he thinks the Athletics are a big zero? Does he want a cinnamon doughnut to go?

And why is he wearing a pink undershirt?

And what the hell is it all supposed to mean anyway?

The back of the card sheds very little light on the situation. In fact, other than telling us that Gus was a radio mechanic in the Navy during the war it is not particularly informative on any matter whatsoever.

Gus Zernial was a member of that band of bulky, slow-moving, power-hitting outfielders of Slavic origin who made their way into the majors shortly after the end of the war. It included among its number Roy Sievers, Clyde Vollmer, Irv Noren, Elmer Valo, and Gil Coan. Of these Gus Zernial was the best. He was also the bulkiest.

Hey Gus, do you know where I can pick up on a pink T-shirt?

Spahn and Sain and a day of rain.

And then Spahn and Sain again and again and again and again and again and again and again and

Someday there will be nostalgia for the seventies, as hard as that may be to realize now.

And when that day comes I intend to be ready.

> Dooley Womack, Rollie Fingers, Phil Roof, Juan Pizarro, Schipio Sphinx, Duke Sims, Ron Swaboda, Randy Hundley, Freddie Patek, Coco Laboy, Manny Mota, Zoilo Versailles

Don McMahon is fifty-four years old.
Rick Reichardt has only one kidney.
Hoyt Wilhelm had his head screwed on sideways.
Denny McLain really did all those things.
And yes, Virginia, "Walt Williams" had no neck.
And his legs weren't particularly long either.

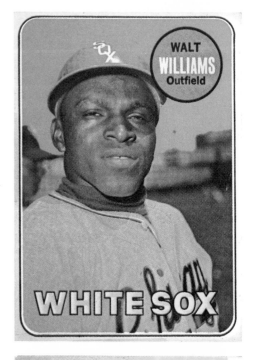

Ted Kazanski was something of a rarity in the majors — a utility infielder who played his entire career with one team. Ted played second, short, and third with the Phillies for six years in the fifties, but was never a starter. Since he never hit over .250, he wasn't much of a pinch hitter either. As a matter of fact, it's difficult to remember exactly what he did in order to earn his salary. A late inning defensive replacement, a pinch runner in a close game — such is the life of the utility player. It must be difficult to keep in shape under such circumstances, much less to keep your spirits up. But Ted Kazanski managed to do both.

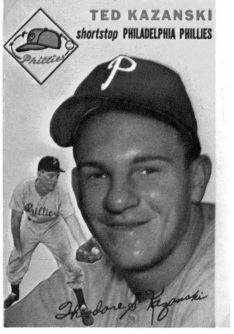

Everybody has their favorite Marv Throneberry joke. Mine was Marv himself.

Then there was the time the Met management, in a laudable if ill-fated attempt to shore up the understandably sagging team morale, threw a birthday party for manager Casey Stengel in the clubhouse between games of a doubleheader loss to the Pittsburgh Pirates. When Marv complained that he had not been given a piece of the birthday cake, Casey leaned over to his disconsolate first baseman and in a voice just loud enough to be heard by every reporter from Great Neck to Canarsie announced, "We wuz gonna give you a piece, Marv, but we wuz afraid you'd drop it."

Then there was the time . . .

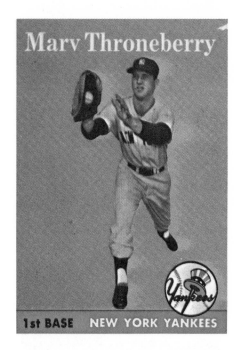

Just wanted to see if you were still paying attention. All kidding aside though, this one is hard to resist. Why do you think Johnny U. looks that way anyway?

Is he stoned?

Is his hair too tight?

Has he just been dropped on his head by Leo Nomellini?

And do my eyes deceive me or is the outline of his skull, from the slope of his jaw to the summit of his brush-cut nerve ends, a perfectly realized set of 90° angles?

Ah, football. A savage business.

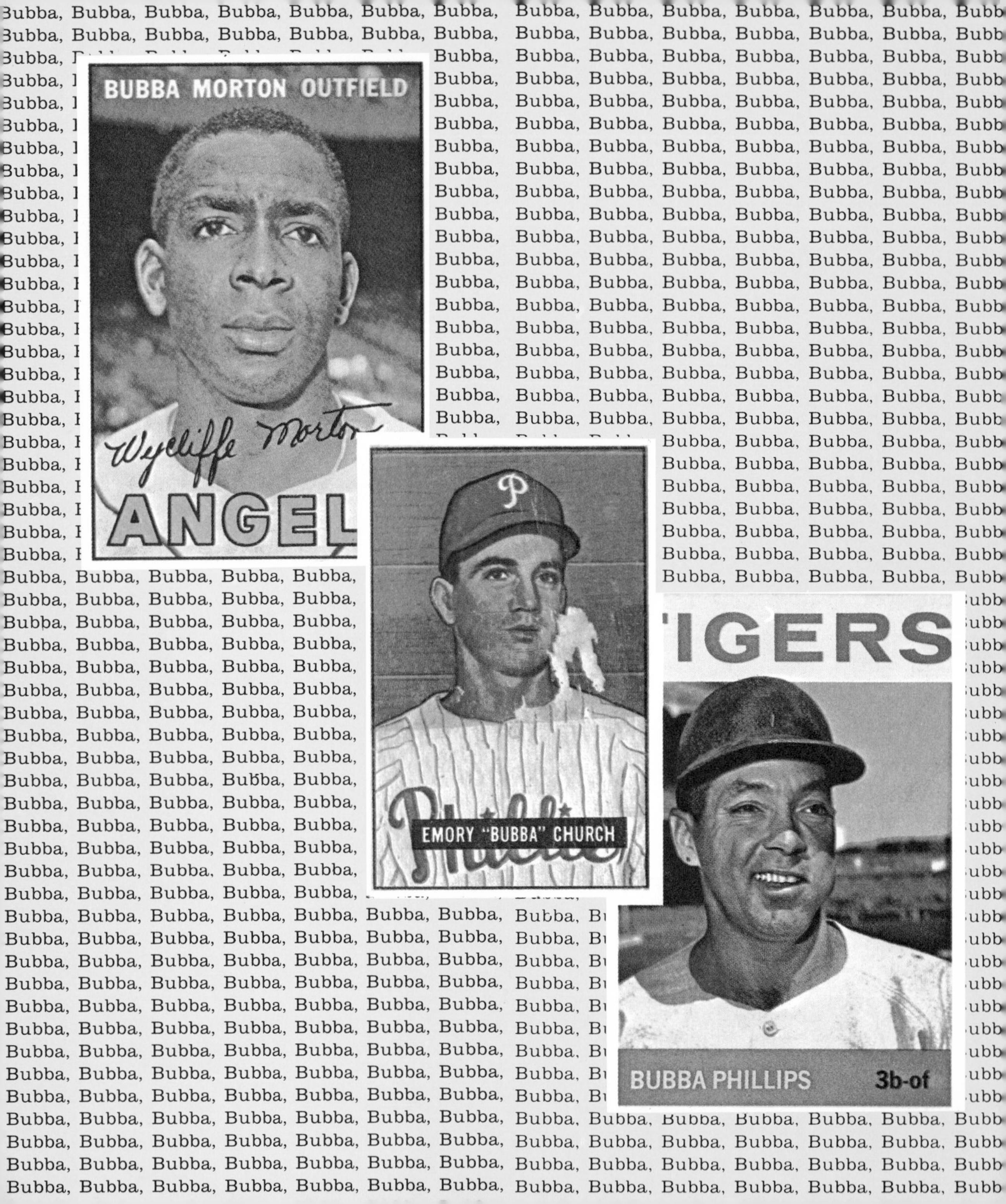

Bubba, Bubba, Bubba, Bubba, Bubba, Bubba, Bubba, Bubba, Bubba, Bubba, Bubba, Bubba, Bubba, Bubba,

BUBBA MORTON OUTFIELD

Wycliffe Morton

ANGEL

EMORY "BUBBA" CHURCH

TIGERS

BUBBA PHILLIPS 3b-of

Bubba, Bubba, Bubba, Bubba, Bubba, Bubba, Bubba, Bubba, Bubba, Bubba, Bubba, Bubba, Bubba, Bubba,

Moe Drabowsky, who grew up collecting baseball cards in Ozanna, Poland, didn't have too many winning seasons as a pitcher for teams in both leagues, but until he joined the Orioles in 1966 (when he finished the season 6-0), he didn't play for many winning teams. Moe was of the Billy Loes school of players—sleepy-looking—but at 6′3″, and with a complicated pitching motion and good stuff, Moe was hard to hit. In what was his greatest single game, in the 1966 World Series, Moe went 6⅔ innings, striking out 11 and getting credit for the win.

In addition to his numerous other accomplishments—none of which come immediately to mind—Jim Delsing was also the pinch runner who replaced Eddie Gaedel, old number ⅛, when that little devil drew a base on balls in his only major league time at bat. Some of the others participating in this poignant and memorable tableau were Frank Saucier, who was lifted—if that's the word I'm looking for—for pinch hitter Gaedel, Bob Cain, who was the pitcher, and Bob Swift, the catcher; for the opposing Detroit Tigers, Zack Taylor, who was little Eddie's manager, Ed Hurly, who was the umpire, and of course Bill Veeck, whose subtle and fiendish imagination gave birth to the entire endeavor. I will spare the rest of the players involved the humiliation of revealing their identities, since, in most cases, if they were standing any further away than third base, they couldn't see what was going on anyway.

How would you like to go through life known as the only man who ever pinch ran for a midget. Huh? Huh? Huh?

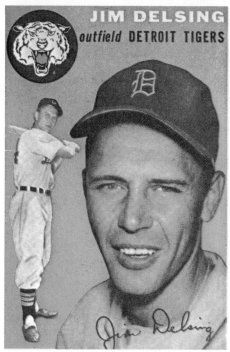

Jim Brosnan was that rarest of athletic types—the intellectual. Or at least he was what passes for an intellectual in the singularly unenlightened area of professional gamesmanship, which of course is not necessarily the same thing. Brosnan made being intelligent respectable among the jocks and, what's more, he made it pay. He was the first of the resident Boswells of the base paths and also probably the best.

In some of the more basic sports—such as hockey, boxing, horse racing and pocket billiards—an intellectual is anybody who can sign an autograph without his business manager's assistance. In the airier climes of professional football and basketball, however, more stringent standards are needed to measure the relative mental capacities of the combatants. Here style is everything, content nothing, so that only the didactic likes of Frank Ryan, the Cleveland Brown quarterback/mathematician whom Chris Schenkel delighted in calling Dr. Ryan, are considered worthy of the lofty title "intellectual." You know, somebody who specializes in wry, self-effacing postgame interviews and takes a lot of graduate courses in the off-season. But in baseball, the great American leveler, the question of a man's intellectual status is a simple matter of deduction: if a player keeps books in his locker then he's an intellectual. If not, not. It makes no difference that the books are by Harold Robbins or Grace Metalious or that they remain unread throughout the entire length of the season; the simple fact of their existence automatically entitles their owner to be considered something of a sage by the sportswriters and to be nicknamed by his teammates "the professor." This is part of American folklore and nobody's ever going to be able to change it. Well, Jim Brosnan not only read all the books in his locker (and there were some pretty hard books in there too); he even went so far as to write a couple himself. In fact, "The Long Season" and "Pennant Race" were the precursors of the seemingly endless stream of diary-style, eavesdropping chronicles of the sporting life which have been pouring down the literary drainspout for the past decade and a half.

On the back of his card we are informed that "Jim writes short stories in his spare time." Now, if that isn't the hallmark of an honest-to-goodness intellectual, I'll be damned if I know what is.

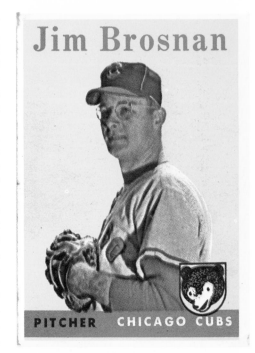

PITCHER   CHICAGO CUBS

Maurice McDermott was Ellis Kinder's drinking partner and the only person in the history of the Poughkeepsie, New York public school system to be chosen unanimously by his High School graduating class as the man most likely to be found dead in a motel room.

If there's one thing baseball has never been short of, it's wise guys. When was the last time you saw a left-handed shortstop anyway? Another funny thing that Joe Koppe did was to change his name from Kopchia (which means schlemiel in Serbo-Croatian) to Koppe (which means schmuck in Alsace-Lorraintian) so that nobody, not even his relatives, knew whether to call him Kopay, Kopee, Cope, or Cop. It didn't matter all that much, of course, since nobody ever had occasion to mention him by name anyway.

To be an athlete's brother is a trial. To be an athlete's son is a sorrow. To be a famous athlete's brother or son is a tragedy. But to be a famous athlete's brother AND son who tries to become a famous athlete himself is just plain foolhardy. Dave Sisler was the son of George Sisler, a Hall of Famer and one of the two or three greatest first basemen who ever lived, and brother of Dick Sisler, whose home run in the last game of the 1950 season clinched the National League Pennant for the Phillies. Do you imagine that there were ever fifteen seconds during the waking existence of Dave Sisler that he was able to forget these facts? What would drive a kid like this to become a ballplayer anyway? Wouldn't he have been happier as a lawyer or a clamdigger or something along that line? He must have known that no matter how good he was he was never going to be good enough. He seemed bright, too. He graduated from Princeton, wore glasses, and was very analytical in postgame interviews. Look at his face in this card — serious, intelligent, taut — the face of an early suicide. Richard Michael Sisler, son of George Harold Sisler, brother of Richard Allan Sisler, possessor of a 38–44 lifetime record, retired from baseball at age thirty-one, wherever you are now, at age forty-two, I only hope that you have made a lot of money in the stock market or are about to discover a cure for cancer.

For your sake.

JOE KOPPE   shortstop

DAVE Sisler
BOSTON RED SOX / PITCHER

Ed Bouchee, from way up in Livingston, Montana, hit the big time with the Phillies in 1956, and batted a respectable .293 as their regular first baseman the next year. A psychological problem, requiring some institutional treatment, kept him out of baseball for most of 1958, and he never regained the form he had had as a rookie. He later played with the Cubs, and, appropriately in terms of his career, finished with the Mets, primarily as a pinch hitter.

Most ballplayers' careers peter out gradually. They get older, their reflexes lose their sharpness, their arteries harden, and they lose that little edge that separates the major leaguer from the common run of humanity. It happened to Cobb and Ruth and DiMaggio. It is happening right now to Willie Mays. Not so though with Rocky Colavito. His was a sudden death, brief and painless, no agonizingly prolonged lingering period for him. In 1965 Rocky hit .287 with 26 home runs for the Cleveland Indians and was probably the best right fielder in the American League. The next year he hit 30 home runs and although his average dipped to .238 he was still one of the most menacing power hitters in all of baseball. In 1967, however, the bottom dropped completely out of the Colavito market. During the next two years Rocky bounced all over the majors—from Cleveland to Chicago to Los Angeles to New York—trying to catch on as a reserve outfielder and pinch hitter, hitting 16 home runs in two seasons and batting .231 and .211 respectively. At thirty-four, this man who had hit 358 home runs (4 in a single game), had driven in an average of 100 runs in eleven major league seasons, and always looked to me like the most promising of promising pubescent rookies, was through. Whatever he once had, he had lost. What once he had been, he was no more.

O Man, place not thy confidence in this present world.

But if you want to talk about a guy whose career just seemed to disintegrate, to come apart at the seams and unravel—slowly, methodically, almost geometrically—like a $35 polyester suit, then Tommy Tresh is definitely your man. In 1962 Tommy was one of the best rookies in the American League. He hit .286, had 20 home runs, 93 RBIs and played both shortstop and the outfield competently, if not spectacularly, for a pennant-winning New York Yankee ball club. He was a college graduate, the son of a former major leaguer, a minor league all star, twenty-five years old, clean cut, a Yankee, and with a name like Tom Tresh can anybody possibly doubt that he was the very epitome of the all-American boy? Well, just to show you that things don't always go by the book, from 1962 to 1968 Tom Tresh's batting average declined almost 100 points from its peak—from .286 to .269 to .246 to .233 to .219 to .195, a neat 20 points a year—and his home-run output fell off from a high of 27 to a low of 11. Now, not even a young Yankee with a name like a movie star and a face like a choirboy can get by on a .195 batting average, even if he is a switch hitter. In 1962 Tom Tresh had everything. He loved the world and the world certainly loved him. By 1968 he didn't have much of anything. He was thirty-one years old; New York was in ninth place (two spots behind the Washington Senators); he was playing in an infield which consisted of Joe Pepitone, Ruben Amaro, and Bobby Cox (the catcher was the immortal Jake Gibbs); he had completely forgotten how to hit; the Yankees were desperately trying to trade him for just about anything. He was even beginning to get crow's feet. All that red-hot potential had turned as cold as a Harry M. Stevens hot dog. Tommy, baby, maybe they made the pants too long.

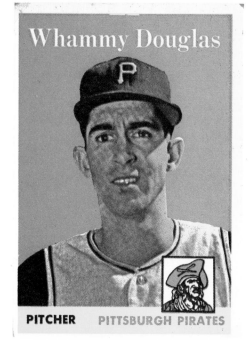

The hat?
 The eyes?
 The name?
 Somebody has definitely got to be pulling our legs with this guy.

It is a common prejudice concerning catchers that they are slow—both with their feet and with their wits. Regarding intelligence, naturally I can't answer for many major league catchers, although I once spoke with Lou Berberet in the Red Sox parking lot and I have seen Johnny Bench on any number of television talk shows, and while neither of these gentlemen has impressed me as a rival to Alfreda Von Nordoff in terms of native mental prestidigitation, I don't think you could exactly call them stupid either. But as far as running is concerned . . . now there you really have something. Major league catchers come in three foot-speeds—slow, slower, and slowest. I have no idea why this is, except that they are generally bulky men, with massive thighs and ample derrieres, who spend a great percentage of their waking hours hunched over and squatting at the knees, a position not exactly conducive to increasing the springing power of the legs. The slowest catchers of recent times have been Bob Tillman, a power-hitting catcher–first baseman with the Red Sox in the early sixties whom I once saw almost thrown out at first from the outfield, Earl Battey, who was a good receiver with the Twins and the White Sox for a dozen years and a rival to John Roseboro in the black Buddah look-alike derby, and Harry Chiti, a reserve catcher with any number of teams over a period of any number of years who looked like everybody's brother-in-law, and played like him too. Fortunately for Harry, his lack of speed was not as noticeable as was the others' because he was such a lousy hitter that he rarely got on base. The only time you really noticed how slow he was was when he was trotting back to the dugout after striking out.

EARL BATTEY   catcher

HARRY CHITI
CLEVE. INDIANS C

Dick Hyde was the last of the legitimate submarine pitchers. Of course Ted Abernathy's still around, but he really throws more of a three-quarter side-arm pitch, whereas Hyde really let it go from way down under. Sometimes, in fact, it looked as though he was throwing the ball from between his legs. Now that I've had some time to think about it, he really wasn't all that good a pitcher, but then again who could have been good with the late fifties' Senators, teams which included on their rosters the likes of Vito Valentinetti, Tex Clevenger, Russ Kemmerer, and Norm Zauchin. And those were some of the stars. Of course throwing the submarine pitch requires an extremely unnatural motion, and before long Hyde had permanently injured his arm trying to scare the living hell out of American League right-handed batters. But he sure was fun to watch while he lasted.

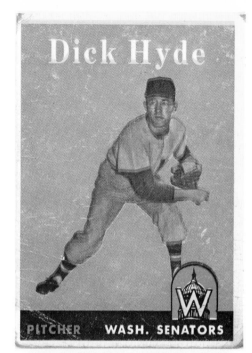

Bob Friend lost an awful lot of games pitching for the Pirates—230—but he did have one 20-game season and several other good ones, and he was a mainstay of the Pirate staff, such as it was, as they fought to stay out of the cellar in the pre-Mazeroski days. Bob was 0–2 in the 1960 Series.

Here they are folks, everybody's favorite double-play combination of the fifties—Chico and Nellie. Chico with his quick glove and his timely base hits, Nellie with his big wad of chewing tobacco and his milk-bottle-handle bat. I used to love to see these two play. They looked so much like kids themselves that they always made me feel like I could step right out of the third row of the bleachers and into the starting lineup. At no time during his entire major league career did Nelson Fox look over thirteen years old. And to make this illusion even stronger, he insisted on wearing his father's old uniforms, which were always at least four sizes too big for him. In truth, Fox was the better ballplayer of the two; he had a life-time .288 batting average and six times hit over .300, playing fourteen years with the White Sox and nine-teen years in the majors overall. But I always had a special place in my heart for Chico, perhaps because of his alliterative nickname (his real name was Alphonso) or because of his peculiarly waiflike ap-pearance, always looking as he did like the wide-eyed Mexican radish-picker that Akim Tamiroff is getting ready to deport. But I think the thing that really assured his place in my affections was his being traded by Chicago in 1956 to make way for Luis Apa-ricio. This was no doubt a smart move on the part of the White Sox, but it made me as mad as hell, indi-cating as it did a certain callous disregard on the part of the Chicago management for Chico, his fam-ily, his friends, and his great legion of loyal ad-mirers, most notably among them myself.

I don't forget easy.

When a manager wants to denigrate one of his pitchers he usually refers to him as a .500 pitcher. This indicates that the pitcher in question does not always deliver his best, that he will lose one for each one that he wins, and that he is constantly letting down the ball club with mediocre performances. In point of fact a pitcher with a .500 record is usually a good pitcher with a lousy ball club or a lousy pitcher with a good ball club. His record will get better or worse depending on the caliber of the teams he plays on. Just to prove that there is such a thing as a .500 pitcher though, we give you: Paul Foytack, whose lifetime won–lost record of 86-87 was neatly divided into indecisive segments such as 15-13, 14-11, 15-13 (he liked that one so much he did it twice), 14-14, 11-10, 10-7, and 5-6. Now, either Foytack had a particularly schizophrenic personality (never being able to go one way without wishing he'd gone another) or he was simply doing his dogged best as a good corporate employee to reflect the true character of the Detroit teams that he played for in the late fifties, teams which consistently finished the season with records like 76-76 (1956), 77-77 (1958), and 76-78 (1959). I choose to believe the latter, trusting as I do in the dauntless and legendary will to win of the resolute professional athlete. The fact that Paul came back in 1964 with the Los Angeles Angels to achieve a record of 0-1, thus placing his career record squarely, securely, and permanently one game under .500, does nothing at all to diminish my faith in this theory.

Jimmy Piersall squirted home plate with water pistols, heaved equipment bags out of dugouts, watered down the infield between innings, ran into walls trying to catch fly balls, threw baseballs at scoreboards and bats at pitchers, practiced sliding during batting practice, slept on the clubhouse floor, bunted with two out and his team six runs behind in the last of the ninth, ran around the bases backward after hitting homers, did sitting-up exercises in the outfield to distract batters, had nervous breakdowns, made comebacks, starred in the movie version of Anthony Perkins' life story, fathered nine children, and in general made life interesting for seventeen of my first twenty-two major league seasons. I miss him.

Every so often there appears a figure on the American sporting scene of such stunning originality and overwhelming vitality that he seems almost singlehandedly to revolutionize an entire sport. Bill Russell revolutionized professional basketball with his awesome defensive improvisations in the pivot. Tod Sloan changed forever the course of thoroughbred horse racing with his monkey on the stick riding style. Otto Graham led professional football away from the cloud of dust running game with his pioneering forward passing technique. And Bobby Orr is even now revolutionizing the game of ice hockey with his rink-length offensive thrusts from the defense. These men by their daring innovation and overpowering skill seem almost to reinvent the very games that they play.

Well that's the way it was with Lou Klimchock too.

For Lou Klimchock by his daring use of the dropped fly and the missed signal, by his unflagging ability to bobble grounders and throw to the wrong base, by his unstinting efforts to strike out in the clutch and ground into double plays, seemed almost singlehandedly and against the greatest possible odds to revitalize baseball ineptitude during the fifties. With his ten-year record of accomplishment — 187 games played (an average of 18 per year), 355 at bats (an average of 35 per year), a .203 lifetime batting average, 41 RBIs and 6 homers, Lou put to rest forever the ridiculously persistent notion that there is no place in the game of baseball for the guy who can't play well. In fact Lou Klimchock can be considered by virtue of his intense and persistent labors on behalf of innovative baseball mediocrity one of the few truly seminal figures in the drab and dreary history of this era. The likes of Julio Becquer, Frank Quillici, Marv Breeding, Bobo Osborne, and Rudy (Rudolph Valentino) Regulado as well as countless other confirmed and inveterate benchwarmers have him to thank for the unwarranted longevity of their careers.

Here's to you Lou. You gave the common fan someone to identify with. You were a constant source of inspiration to all us bumblers. It makes one feel good just to sit here and think about you.

LOU
KLIMCHOCK
WASH. SENATORS   INF.

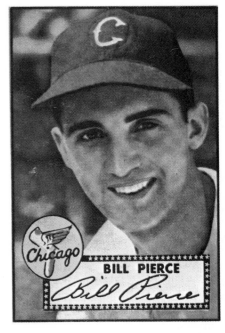

BILL PIERCE

I would guess that I saw the Chicago White Sox play about three dozen times during the course of the fifties, and every single time Billy Pierce was the starting pitcher. I don't know whether this was because the White Sox management overused little Billy or because I just happened to show up when it was his turn in the starting rotation, but as far as I was concerned Billy Pierce was the only pitcher the White Sox had. Chicago made one of the best trades of recent memory in 1949 when they swapped their mediocre second baseman Don Kollaway to the Tigers for the left-handed Pierce. Billy went on to win about two-hundred games for the White Sox over the next thirteen years while Kolloway lasted only three seasons with the Tigers, batting .265 with 9 home runs. This deal ranks right up there with Richie Allen for Tommy John, Nick Buonoconti for Kim Hammond, and Francis Gary Powers for Rudolph Abel in the register of all-time, one-for-one swindles. So you see kids, you **can** get something for nothing after all.

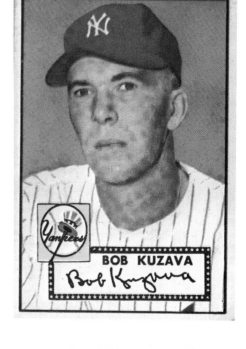

Bob Kuzava played with a lot of teams in his ten years in the big leagues, but his shining moment came, as it frequently does to even the most inept athlete, when he pitched in the seventh game of the 1952 World Series for the Yankees, and retired the last eight Dodgers to preserve a slim two-run victory margin in the last game of one of the most exciting World Series ever.

Sal Maglie was nicknamed "The Barber," among other things, for his proclivity toward moving batters back and away from the plate with high, inside fast balls. Also, he could have used a barber to hold back his heavy, sinister beard, which made him look tougher than he possibly could have been. On the mound for the New York Giants in the early fifties, though, he was tough. He went 23–6 in 1951, and over the course of ten seasons as a starting pitcher with a number of teams in both leagues, he was 119–62, for the ninth-best pitching percentage in baseball history, .657.

BILL CONSOLO infield *BOSTON RED SOX*

Someday I'd like to sit down and have a long talk with
a major league scout about how and why he makes a
decision to sign a particular juvenile prospect.
Around about 1952 the Red Sox shelled out 90,000
balloons, which at that time was a record for them, for
the services of a hot-shot kid third baseman from
Cleveland named Billy Consolo who was supposed to
be the greatest thing since sliced bread. The story on
him was that he could hit, run, field, throw, bunt,
slide, had power, and was smart. Well, he was smart
all right, smart enough to get 90 grand out of Tom
Yawkey, but as far as the other qualities were concerned, I'm afraid the realities of the situation did not
quite live up to the expectations. He could hit, but not
breaking pitches. He could run, but seldom got the
chance. He had a great glove but was extremely erratic and his arm was so highly undisciplined that
most of his throws ended up at least six rows into the
boxes behind the first base bag. About his bunting
and sliding prowess I'll have to suspend judgment. It
seems to me that any twelve-year-old kid with an
ounce and a half of common sense could have told
you after fifteen minutes of watching Billy in action
that although he possessed a stunning array of
native athletic abilities he was never going to be a
halfway decent major league ballplayer because all of
those attributes were deeply and irrevocably flawed
and because there was no sense of balance or coordination between the flawed and the unflawed compo-
nents. Which is to say that if you are starting out to

construct a large cantaloupe, the best thing to have is a small cantaloupe and not a collection of large cantaloupe parts. More often than not the parts don't fit.

But the clinker to end all clinkers in the great floating bonus-baby crap game was Dave Nicholson. In 1959 the Baltimore Orioles, in the throes of a disastrously conceived rebuilding program, gave young Mr. Nicholson upwards of $200,000 in cold hard cash to sign a contract with their Knoxville team in the Class B Sally League. The line on Dave was that he could hit the ball a mile, which was true—when he could hit it at all, which was seldom. In two years with the Orioles, Dave hit .359 . . . **cumulatively**—.186 one year and .173 the next. He also struck out once every three trips to the plate. Well, you didn't have to hit the Baltimore management over the head to prove to them that this was not much of a return on their capital investment, and so they wrote Dangerous Dave off as a tax loss and shipped him off to the White Sox in an egg crate. Here he proceeded to hit 22 very long home runs, bat .229, and set a major league record by striking out 175 times in one year. There followed short stints at Houston and Atlanta in the National League before Dave's seven-year odyssey in search of the perfect fast ball finally came to an end. In seven major league seasons Dave was at bat 1,419 times and hit 61 home runs. Unfortunately he also struck out 573 times. To put this in its proper perspective one must realize that Nelson Fox, who was in the majors for nineteen years and was at bat over 9,000 times, seven times as often as Nicholson, had only 213 career strike-outs, about 40 percent of Nicholson's seven-year total, and even Mickey Mantle, who holds the all-time strike-out record of 1,710—about three times Nicholson's total—required six times his total at bat to achieve this distinction. Also Mantle's ratio of base on balls to strike-outs was 1-1, about right for the average power hitter, while Nicholson's was 1-2½ or 213-573. One could go on and on, of course, but the plain ugly truth of the matter is that Dave Nicholson did not really belong in the major leagues at any time, and that if general managers in both leagues had not insisted on trying to turn his $200,000 bonus into a self-fulfilling prophesy, he never would have stayed up for more than fifteen minutes.

OUTFIELD
DAVE NICHOLSON

No perfection is so absolute
That some impurity doth not pollute.
— William Shakespeare
"The Rape of Lucrece"

HARVEY HADDIX
Pitcher

Pittsburgh
Pirates

Well, Bill, you certainly weren't just whistling up your sleeve with that one, as Harvey Haddix no doubt can confirm. It was Harvey's curious fate—call it destiny or ill fortune if you will—to reach the very apex of earthly perfection: a hitless, errorless, walkless pitching performance on the very night (July 12, 1959), that his teammates on the Pittsburgh Pirates had chosen to go without scoring a run. Harvey pitched 12 innings of flawless baseball, retiring 36 Milwaukee batters in succession only to lose in the bottom half of the 13th on the only Brave hit of the game. By this stroke of calamitous ill fortune he thus became the only pitcher in major league history to lose a perfect game.

From that evening on Harvey, who was known for his fine fielding as "The Kitten," wore the baleful and painfully contrived smile he displays for you here as part of his regular uniform. He bought it used from Roman Mejias and had it surgically attached by Tommy Byrne. It is the reluctantly self-deprecating smile of the perennially dumped-on, the wry smile of the universal victim, the man who expects very little of his peers and knows secretly that he's going to have to settle for quite a good deal less.

OSSIE CHAVARRIA • INF

ATHLETICS

Ossie Chavarria was the Panamanian Tito Francona.

142

Everybody knows Joe, Dom, and Vince DiMaggio, Felipe, Matty, and Jesus Alou, Clete, Cloyd and Ken Boyer, Tony and Billy Conigliaro, Phil and Joe Niekro.

But how many of you remember Dave and Dennis Bennett, Frank and Milt Bolling, Gene and George Freese, Granny and Wesley Hamner, Hal and George Jefcoat, George and Everett Kell, Alex and Walter Kellner, Richard and Marty Keough, Billy and Bobby Klaus, Lindy and Von McDaniel, Rene and Marcel Lachmann, Frank and Al Lary, Bob and Bill Lillard, Marty and Johnny Marion, Chi Chi and Freddy Olivo, Hank and Eddie Sauer, Bobby and Wilmer Shantz, Norm and Larry Shery, and Wally and Jimmy Westlake.

My favorite baseball playing brothers of the fifties were Ted, Ed and Bob Sadowski, Mike and Jim Baxes, and Solly and Sammy Drake.

Whatever they had brother—it ran in the family.

With the possible exception of Jonas Salk, John Foster Dulles, and Annette Funicello, no one public figure so personified the fifties for me as did Vic Power. He was a line-drive-hitting first baseman for the Athletics and the Indians all through that glorious somnambulant decade who held his bat like a stalk of bananas, caught everything with one-handed disdain, and always managed to hit around .300 no matter how many times they tried to knock him down. I don't know what it was exactly that made Vic stick out above all those other ruggedly ostentatious individualists—Frank Sullivan, Alex Kellner, et al. Suffice to say that no one ever hit such frozen ropelike liners, assumed such a novel and menacing stance in the batter's box, was so deft and light-footed around the first-base bag, swore so mightily at umpires and hecklers, or possessed a more novel approach to the game than did Mr. Victor Pellot Power of Arecibo, Puerto Rico.

Wherever you may be now Vic—let it all hang out.

If the Yankees were the bullying big brothers of the American League and the Red Sox the pesky little brothers. If the Tigers were the kindly elderly uncles and the Indians the nervous bumbling fathers. If the Browns were the stupid distant cousins and the Athletics the annoying brothers-in-law. Then the Senators were the obnoxious little nephews and the White Sox the fussy fretting aunts. The White Sox had great pitching, great speed, great defense, great hustle and the most anemic and ineffectual hitting this side of the Pioneer League. For this reason most of their games were decided by 1 run, and they always came in second in the American League. For the White Sox 2 walks, an error, and a stolen base constituted a rally. A 2-run victory was tantamount to a rout. Another thing you might remember about the pale hose was that all of their outfielders were named Jim. Jim Busby, Jim Rivera, Jim Landis—Jim Delsing, Jim McAnary, Jim Lenhardt—Jim Mele, Jim Hirshberger, Jim Minoso. Even Johnny Groth's real name was Jim, until he changed it for esthetic reasons.

Don Drysdale was, like Johnny Podres, a career Dodger, and one of the best pitchers in the league for many years. With Sandy Koufax, Don was the chief starter for the Dodgers. At 6′5″, and with an elaborate windup, Don had a very effective fastball, and accumulated the eighth-best career strike-out record in baseball: 2,462 over thirteen years. Altogether he pitched 3,369 innings, and still, at the end of his career, he had enough on the ball to throw 8 shutouts.

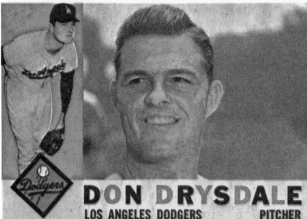

There are some ballplayers who should not be traded. Ralph Kiner, for instance, should not have been traded, nor Hank Greenberg, nor certainly not Rogers Hornsby. In this category I would also place Dizzy Trout, Hal Newhouser, and Ed Bailey, not just because they were good ballplayers but because they represented something about the times in which they played and the teams for which they did their playing. This brings me to the case of Hank Bauer—who never should have been allowed to wander more than seventy-five miles from the Copacabana. All during the fifties, from 1948 to 1960 in fact, Hank Bauer **was** the New York Yankees to me. The Yankees certainly had better all-around players during this period— Mantle, Berra, Rizzuto, Howard; even Bill Skowron and Tony Kubek possessed greater natural skills—but somehow or other none of them wore the pinstripes as well as Bauer, none of them really personified to me the proud Yankee tradition of Ruth, Gehrig, Huggins, and Dickey. When Hank was traded to Kansas City in 1960 as part of the Roger Maris deal, I could not and would not believe it. And when I went out to the ball park several weeks later to see Kansas City play, I had, right there in section 306B of the right field grandstand, what amounted to a minor identity crisis. Who was that man playing right field for the Athletics and calling himself Hank Bauer? He isn't even wearing a Yankee uniform, for God's sake. It was a little like coming home from school and finding my mother dressed up in combat fatigues.

145

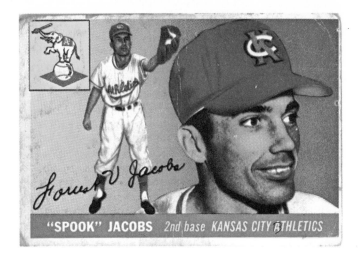

"SPOOK" JACOBS   2nd base KANSAS CITY ATHLETICS

I don't know, you tell me.

Some things are just funny in and of themselves. They require little or no explanation, and are in fact most often beyond analysis. In this category I would place – the Edsel, Sonny Tufts, the prune danish, Dr. Joyce Brothers, Orange Julius, Metrecal, Keye Luke, Levittown, Wayne Newton, the wombat, the Hadassah, Guam, Tony Leonetti, Gatorade, Mrs. Paul's Fish Sticks, Bosco, Kate Smith, Carmen Lombardo, gerbils, Robby the Robot, Latvia, Geritol, Earl Scheib, Philadelphia, Harold Stassen, Grossinger's, the Flugel horn, Tidy Bowl, and Costa Rica.

The list of ballplayers in this category is just about limitless. But Guido Grilli is certainly a good beginning. Then there was Nelson Chitholm, Ernio Fazio, Purnel Goldy, Stuffy Sternweiss, Buster Narum, and Bobo Osborne. Not to mention the Chicago Cubs of 1952. And the entire National League in 1957. I'm sure you have some favorite of your own. Arlan Bockhorn? Bruno Horvath? Ralph Guglielmi?

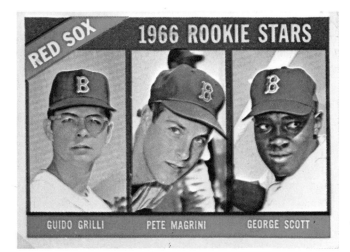

RED SOX   1966 ROOKIE STARS

GUIDO GRILLI   PETE MAGRINI   GEORGE SCOTT

146

Some Final Observations
on Trading, Hoarding, Collecting
and Other Aberrations
of the Baseball Card Life

Your mother threw your baseball cards out, right?

Your own mother.

I know. I know.

But good God, man, try to pull yourself together.

You're never going to get to glide down the Grand Canal with Vera Ellen, get your crewcut to stand up straight with Butch Wax, or play center field in the House that Ruth built.

So why worry about something as trivial as a few baseball cards?

I know. I know.

You put them in a cigar box in your closet with about two hundred rubber bands around them. All face up and lovingly alphabetized and camouflaged with about fifteen pounds of sweat socks. And your mother found them, didn't she? She never looked in that closet before, did she? Except the time that you bought those dirty pictures. But she certainly got in there good that day. And threw your childhood right into the trash can. Into the scrap heap with the bacon fat and the Kleenex. Along with the pencil box you had made out of Popsicle sticks. Your youth. Right out with the back issues of **Pageant.** And never mind that you were twenty-six years old at the time. Or that you hadn't looked at them in almost fifteen years. You knew they were there, and that was enough. Enough to get you through another winter.

And your mother threw them away.

Your very own mother.

Well that's the way it is with all of us, kid.

That's what mothers are for after all.

There are four things that everybody remembers about baseball cards:

The pale chalky powder that clung to them interminably. On your fingers, on your shirt cuffs, in your hair. Bubble gum dust.

That you could never get a Ted Williams, no matter how hard you tried.

That you could never **not** get a Cliff Mapes, no matter how hard you tried.

And that your mother threw them out one sunny summer morning. And there was no possible way to get them back.

There a number of other things that everybody remembers about baseball cards too, but fortunately I have managed to forget them.

Hoarding: Say I had a card I knew my friend needed in order to complete a particular set. And say I had doubles of that card. Well, I could just about name my price now couldn't I? And being an average American kid I was prepared to drive a pretty hard bargain. Why not give this friend the card, you ask? Out of a sense of friendship and brotherhood, you say? And let him be the first one on the block to have a complete set? Better you should give him first choice of your Christmas gifts, still wrapped and gleaming silently under the tree. Collecting baseball cards was serious stuff after all, like collecting stocks or money or porcelain snuff boxes. Except that with baseball cards you could have so much more fun — playing games with them, reading their backs, dipping them in paraffin. This last an illegal aid to serious flipping.

Individual cards were not important because of the player whose picture appeared on them, of course, or because of his actual baseball reputation, but rather for the difficulty you encountered in getting hold of him. Some cards actually appeared so frequently that after a while they became a joke. You'd accumulate so many of them that you'd have to begin throwing them away. I remember one year, 1955 I think, when I must have had fifteen Mickey Mantles. You couldn't even use him for flipping because no one wanted another Mickey Mantle. Everyone on my block was thoroughly sick of Mickey Mantle. And that was long before such emotions had become popular.

Trading: On the other hand, there were the cards that nobody had, except for some kid who visited your house with his parents, and who brought along some (or all) of his cards, probably to look at and to play with in the car. And this kid, whom you didn't like from the start, had number 303, which was somebody like Milo Candini, who pitched with the 1951 Phillies. Your dislike for this kid quickly turned to hatred as it silently became clear to him that you wanted Milo Candini, and he wasn't going to let you have him. Not unless you had something he wanted equally as bad. But you never did. You might try to impress him with some of your lead soldiers or your metal warehouse with the miniature boxes of F & F coughdrops that fit into the trucks that pulled up to the loading platform. But the kid would always go home with that beautiful card of Milo Candini. And you'd never be able to get it, no matter how many nickels you spent, and that was one of the principal joys of collecting baseball cards. As well as one of its principal sorrows.

Collecting: These bartering rituals are far from a dead art of course. A lively market in yellowing pasteboards still persists. Kept flourishing by balding refugees from the fifties — aging acolytes at the altar of Stan Hack.

Throughout the country there are scores of clubs, newsletters, conventions, and thousands of otherwise sane individuals all devoted to baseball and other sports memorabilia. Most serious collectors advertise their specific needs in periodicals like "The Sports Hobbyist," P.O. Box 3731, Detroit, Michigan 48205. ("Will trade EXCELL PIEDMONT-SWEET CAPORAL SET for TOPPS BLUE BACKS or selected

150

AMERICAN CARAMEL series.") They know what they want all right, be it an extremely rare Cracker Jacks reprint of Frank "Home Run" Baker or a Cloyd Boyer action shot from the Kahn Frankfurter Company ("The Wiener the World Awaited"). They are as serious in their own way as collectors of coins or stamps are in theirs, specifying the condition of cards they have for sale in much the same way as antiquarian booksellers describe their offerings—"mint, worn but generally good," etc. These nostalgic packrats never seem to throw anything away, and card collections numbering in the tens of thousands are as commonplace as a Buddy Blattner error. One collector with whom we have communicated, Bruce York of Wholesale Cards in Georgetown, Connecticut, claims to have a current inventory of ten million cards.

Bruce, Bruce, can you hear us, Bruce?

The best place to witness this nostalgic phenomenon in action though is at a card collectors' annual convention. Many of the card crazies in attendance rent space on the convention floor in order to sell or trade their antediluvian treasures: extinct sports magazines, moldering press guides and yearbooks, single game programs, or unused tickets to the 1955 Rose Bowl. The amount of haggling and kvetching at such fetes and the scope of the antiquities on display is beyond even your wildest childhood fantasies—cards from every imaginable cigarette company are represented. Mecca, Hassan Cork Tips, Red Man Tobacco, Polar Bear, Old Judge, Turkey Red. The cards of Allen and Ginter cigarettes featuring illustrations of "pugilists," oarsmen, wrestlers, pool players, rifle shooters, and club swingers—whatever that is—as well as our beloved baseball players. Talk of the Diamond reprints from 1909. Play Ball Gum cards from the late thirties. Giveaways from "Sporting Life" magazine, 1911 ("The Magazine That Made Baseball Popular. 5¢ the copy"). Cards from Mothers Cookies in 1952, with a complete set of Pacific Coast League players. Lummis Peanut Butter cards from Philadelphia. Glendale Meat Company Cards, 1953 (blood stained and liver smelling Detroit Tigers going for $12 apiece on the convention floor). "The Sports Hobbyist" regularly reports on all these doings, and certain collectors like Frank Nagy of Detroit have achieved almost superstar status—wheeler-dealers in white on white acetate shirts grinning out at you from behind their wooden sales stalls ("Larry Pfeister, the genial milkman from Skokie, Illinois, shares a laugh with fellow collector Felix Phillips at a recent hobbyist get together"). It's enough to set you rummaging back through your attic—a fortune to be made in torn and mildewed Elbie Fletchers.

Some of the more prominent dealer/collectors we have come in contact with are: The Card Collectors Company, Box 293, Franklin Square, New York 11010; Gar Miller, 400 W. Cherry St., Wenonah, N.J. 08090; Glen Lewis, 3535 De Kalb Ave., Bronx, N.Y. 10467.

These gentlemen will be glad to help you should you be interested in starting a collection. Don't bother to write to us about it though. Our mothers threw all our cards out.

Goodnight Sibbi Sisti, wherever you are.